MORE THAN RICE

Pamala Kennedy Chestnut

ISBN: 978-0-88144-263-2

Foreword

Pamala Chestnut is an extraordinary human being, bringing together a life history of overcoming in almost every arena of life. She is an extraordinary speaker, writer, sought after guest on talk shows; radio and television and life coach to hundreds whom she has inspired. However, Pamala has gained her status not because of her positions she has held or the awards she has won, but because of the scars she has overcome—physically, mentally, and emotionally—in her journey to becoming one of America's most beloved inspirational women. Let Pamala inspire you in her first novel on the subject of human trafficking, "*More Than Rice*"…you will not be disappointed.

Lance Lee, PhD
Executive Coach and Consultant
Director, Center of Relationship
Silicon Valley, California

Contents

Part One: Chosen

I LONGED for a cool breeze as I pulled at my hair sticking to the back of my neck. My cotton blouse was soaked with perspiration. Today is more humid than usual in Manila, but September is always intolerable. I wish Miguel would hurry up—where is my big brother anyway? He said 6:00 P.M. *sharp*. I left the dress shop a few minutes early to make certain he would not have to wait. He is always so impatient with me; says that Papa favors me. Maybe so, but what if he does, I am the youngest of nine and must exist on everyone else's hand-me-downs. I hate it! This is the very reason I am working at Miss Lolani's Dress Shop. I want a new dress of my very own. *It will be red,* she thought, *No, blue…with puff sleeves. That is, if there is any money left after Papa takes what is needed for the family.*

Papa works hard with Uncle Tula farming rice, but what he makes is never enough for the entire family to live on. He says every year it costs more just to feed all of us. However, lately, he has been encouraged by the promises of our newly elected president, President Estrada! Everyone likes him, it seems. He has pledged to help the poor and farmers in particular. Papa is very optimistic. So, maybe I will get my new dress soon.

Gabriela's thoughts were interrupted by a well-dressed Caucasian man walking toward her. He stared so brazenly it was somewhat uncomfortable for her.

"Good evening, Miss. I apologize for staring, but I could not help it—really! You are stunningly attractive. Taller than most Filipino girls, aren't you?" I did not know if I should answer him, but I managed a smile for the compliment he'd given.

"It's getting rather late, are you waiting for someone to pick you up?" I felt it was time to answer him; I had to be polite, didn't I?

"Uh, yes. Actually, I am waiting for my brother. He is coming soon, and he is never late." I lied.

The man looked toward the busy street and waved. Suddenly, a car pulled up beside us and stopped. What happened next was a blur. I vaguely remember a man opening the rear car door. He then stepped onto the walkway and grabbed me. Violently, he shoved me into the car. I screamed in terror while trying to reach the door, but my hand was knocked away. He then placed a gun to my head.

The man driving turned and said, "Remember, she is not to be harmed. No blemish was the requirement. Now, just quiet her down until we get further away!" I felt the sting of the man's anger lingering on my hand. My stomach was churning and I felt as if I would be sick. What just happened? Where are they taking me, and why?

All at once, there was a sharp pain in my arm followed by warmth throughout my body. I cannot remember getting out of the car or being placed in the room that I am now in;

nevertheless, I am here. The reality of this strange place makes it apparent that it's not just a horrible nightmare that I am waking up from. After a few moments, I realize that my hands and feet are bound and my mouth is gagged. I hear voices coming from someplace nearby. It is clearly male voices speaking Spanish. I can make out a few words here and there. My grandmother, Nuna, often spoke in Spanish, like many of the older generation did in Manila, during her youth.

What are the words they keep repeating, *novia vergin*, "young girl?" No, I think it is virgin bride. Who are they referring to, is this me? Am I going to be someone's bride? The horror of the thought stunned me; these men have taken me for the precise purpose of becoming someone's bride! *Someone?* A stranger! A horrible man; he must be despicable to resort to this way of acquiring a bride for himself. A bride is not what he wants. He wants a slave, someone taken against her will.

How did this happen? Gabriela's thoughts began to retrace her steps. *I left work, and then walked a few blocks to wait for Miguel. He said to wait on the walkway of the Luzon Expressway. I recall it being very warm even though it was already 6:00 P.M. There was a lot of traffic on the Luzon, so many cars: which one stopped for me? Why did they choose me? Why, oh why, did they choose me? Who was the man who spoke to me? Did he look familiar at all? Could I have tried harder and escaped? I must quiet my thoughts or my brain will explode.*

I do not even know how I got from the car to the cot in this small dark room. There is nothing I can see in the shadows but this one uncomfortable old cot. I buried my head into the sham of a bed and cried. I sobbed, pleaded, and prayed for someone to help me. I do remember the Sisters at church saying that God would help if I simply asked.

"God!" I sobbed pitifully, "If there is a God, where are You now? How could You allow this to happen to me?"

Exhausted and still partially drugged, I began to drift off to sleep. Feeling alone and hopeless, my thoughts all of a sudden turned to my family; they must be terrified. By now, Miguel has surely gone to the dress shop to inquire as to my whereabouts. They will tell him I left and certainly, he and my family will desperately start searching for me. It is my only hope!

Exhausted, Gabriela fell into a restless sleep.

Home

Miguel drove back and forth in front of the walkway off the Luzon. "My sister! Where is that girl? If she only knew of all the evils that could happen to a young lady alone, she would wait where I instructed her to." Her beauty could be a curse instead of a blessing.

There have been rumors of girls being stolen and sold into human trafficking right here in Manila. Gabriela's exceptional beauty had been apparent since she was very young. Why, even Grandmother Nuna named her *Gabriela* because she was so beautiful. I remember her saying the day she was born, "The angel Gabriel sent her and blessed her with rare beauty – we need to name her after him."

Gabriela was born with flawless golden brown skin and large almond shaped brown eyes; even as a baby, they seemed to dance with fire. Her smile revealed perfect white teeth, which was considered a divine gift to a Filipino. Gabriela's looks and bouncy personality allowed her preferential treatment at times, especially from Papa. Her energetic, playful flirtations were considered innocent and passed off as actions of an immature child. *But now*, thought Miguel, She is almost seventeen years old; she needs to be more responsible for her behavior. Especially since her tall lanky body transformed, she now has the body of a woman—not a child! I have had to protect her good name against crude jokes this entire past year," Miguel mumbled defensively. "And now she places herself in danger by wandering around at this time of day on the streets of Manila. Not to mention wasting my time searching for her during the busiest time of the day!"

Miguel finally gave up looking for Gabriela on the walkway and headed for Miss Lolani's Dress Shop. It took a long time just to find a place to park. Annoyed, he slammed the car door and walked to the shop only to find a CLOSED sign hanging on the door. "Great!" he said out loud. He peered through the window and saw Miss Lolani speaking to an older woman, an affluent customer no doubt. He knocked at the window until he got her attention. She said something to the customer and walked toward the shop door.

"We are closed, Miguel, what do you need?"

"I am looking for my sister, is she still here by chance?"

"No! She left over an hour ago. She said she was to meet you and did not want to be late, said something about not wanting to anger you again."

Miguel apologized for the interruption and left.

He then decided she must have given up waiting for him and found a ride home with a friend. "Yes, that's just like her to take off with a friend, even though she knew I would show up and be worried about her." Having reached this conclusion, Miguel turned his car toward home, secretly praying his impression was a right one.

Papa looked at his watch and called to his wife in the kitchen, "Are you putting their dinner away?"

"Yes, but this is later than they have ever been, I pray they did not get into an accident," her voice sounded worried.

"I am sure they are fine, it is more than likely that old Jeep of Miguel's has once again broken down somewhere along the way home. He will fix it and soon, they will drag themselves in worn out and starved." Papa wanted to sound reassuring, but he feared his words could not cover up his own worry. He then got up and walked outside, saying he needed some fresh air; in truth, he could not bear just sitting there, worried and wondering where they could be so late. Each time car lights appeared on the street, his eyes glared in desperate hope, praying it would be his children—both of them.

Miguel's thoughts were all over the place during the lengthy drive home. "What if she is not there? What if something has happened to her?" It made him angry, worried, and scared—scared to tell his Papa that he quite possibly lost his baby daughter. Losing a daughter is certainly news that would cause any parent to grieve. But Gabriela was not just a daughter to his Papa. Miguel then spoke the painful words out loud to give them their unmitigated power, "Out of all of his kids, she is his favorite." Miguel frantically began to conjure up various versions of a defense, but none seemed convincing enough to defer his pending fate if Gabriela was not safe at home.

Refreshment

Gabriela was awakened by the sound of a key unlocking the door to her room—*her* room? How meaningless were these words now? So many times throughout her young life, she longed for her very own room. She complained often and pouted over the fact that she had to share a room with four sisters. One could scarcely call it a room; it didn't even have a wall separating them from the area her brothers slept in. It was merely a curtain her mom had made to give them some semblance of privacy. Gabriela loved her family, but there never seemed to be enough of anything—room or food.

Papa did try to provide for us, but our family was so big. All of our relatives and friends have large families but no one seems to be able to truly care for them well. I decided when I was very young that I did not want to continue this way of life, a life with never enough. My sister Paula said if I did not marry and did not have a lot of children, I would not make God and the Church happy.

So, is this kidnapping a punishment for my desires? Have I truly made God mad at me? Can I confess and be rescued? I closed my eyes and tried, but knew my confession was not genuine. Then I said softly, "I can't do this; God surely knows when a person is lying just to get out of trouble." I was getting angry at myself for even thinking about God right now. "I don't know why I continue bringing up the subject of God. He clearly has no regard for me. Why should I even consider what He does or does not like?"

Alone and afraid, Gabriela lay on the cot quietly thinking of the implications of this conclusion.

The door opened and two men entered the room. One man walked toward me; he looked me over then pulled me up from the cot. He untied my feet, and then removed the gag.

He placed his hand over my mouth and said, "If you want refreshment, do not make a sound; otherwise, I will gag you again." I was not hungry, but was desperately thirsty. The other man placed a plate of what looked like rice on the floor, next to it was a small bowl of water.

One of the men nodded his head in the direction of the wall across from me, and then pointed to a small can. "To relieve yourself, do not stink up the place, either!" They both left with no explanation as to how I was to eat and drink since my hands remained tied. "So they intend for me to get on my knees and eat like a dog?" For an instant, I thought, *There is no way I am going to lower myself to that level*, but my parched tongue won over my pride.

Slowly, I rose from the cot; with my hands tied behind my back, I walked toward the water. I awkwardly fell to my knees and began lapping the water like our dog Joey at home. Tears flowed down my face into the water I was drinking. With my heart and pride broken, I got up and returned to the cot. It had somehow become my only comfort.

I lay quiet for what seemed like hours, but in reality, it probably was not more than a few minutes since the men had brought me what they referred to as refreshment. During these drawn out moments of silence, I tried hard to think of something from home, anything to get my mind off of what was happening. Happy thoughts fill my mind: of Papa and how much he loves to fish and the times he took me along. Once, we even got to ride a Ro-Ro to go fishing near Cebu City. Papa was a happy man who loved teasing each of us and making us laugh even when we had little to laugh about. Then I whispered, "His heart will break when he realizes I am not coming home tonight."

What about my mother? With eight other children to think of today, she may not even notice I am missing. I am pretty certain that I am her least favorite. I asked her once why she had so little love and praise for me; she just laughed and said, "You get what is left over after raising eight others, Gabby." Then she would get a sad look on her face; I think she was remembering my sister, Dalisay. She died a year or so after I was born. I did not know her, of course, but I heard many times from Grandmother Nuna that Dalisay was the sweetest, kindest girl you could ever meet. I wonder now how she died. No one ever wanted to speak of it much, but now, I am so alone and maybe, the fear of dying myself has me wondering how it happened.

Gabriela's thoughts were interrupted by the sound of the door opening. This time, there was a third man accompanying the other two. Gabriela peered at him through the dark, and then thought to herself, *I recognized this man! He is the one who grabbed me from the street.* He then came near to me and insisted that I stand up.

As I stood, he pushed me down, "Stand, I said. What is wrong with you, stupid girl?" I stood up again only to be pushed back onto the cot. "You are so high and mighty now aren't you, too good to eat the refreshment sent to you?" Dare I answer him? I remained silent. "Now, you listen to how this will work best for you. If you want to live and follow the destiny chosen for you, you are to eat *what* we bring to you, *when* we bring it to you. Is this understood, dirty little Princess?" I just nodded my head yes, which seemed the safer way to answer.

9

"You need to eat now; we leave shortly to take you to another 'Palace,' little Princess." Then he threw his head back and laughed mockingly. As they left the room, one of the men glanced back at me and looked intently into my eyes; his eyes were almost pleading with me to listen and obey. I walked over to the plate on the floor, managed to get down on my knees and began eating the rice with my mouth from the plate.

The Transfer

The door opened again, and though I did not know it at the time, it would be the last time I would see this particular door open. The two men were there to take me to the next *palace*. One of them walked to the cot and pulled me to my feet. The kinder of the two once again stared into my eyes as he placed the gag through my mouth, and then tied it behind my head. This time, he would also blindfold me. His touch was not one of torture and cruelty, it almost felt as if he were preparing me for a child's game of hide and seek. But this was not a kind action for sure. It was not a game, and if I were a child when I came here tonight, I am no longer one.

I stumbled trying to keep up with my escorts; we walked through the building and out a door into the warm September air. What seemed a nuisance earlier today had now become sheer pleasure. I took a deep breath. "Ah, to breathe fresh air regardless of the temperature was wonderful! The air feels a little cooler on my face, so it must be very early in the morning. If I were honest, I would have to admit I took a lot for granted every day of my life—simple things like being able to breathe the air outside, leave a room, or use my hands to eat. Or to sleep in a safe place, regardless of how crowded it was…why was I so ungrateful? I miss all of them terribly!

We got into a car and drove for what I think was about an hour. Still blindfolded, I was told to get out of the car. One of the men, I am assuming the one who gagged me, gave me instructions as to which way to slide out of the car; he then held my arm tight, steadying me when I began to sway a little. Any kindness now shown to me, regardless of how small, was welcomed. Once out of the car, I could smell the salty sea air and knew I was about to board some type of boat. My thoughts soon were proven correct as my feet felt the unsteady suspension bridge beneath them. I knew this kind of bridge was used to get people aboard a vessel of some kind. My heart sank when I realized I was truly leaving Manila. It would take nothing short of a miracle for me to ever see my family again.

Once on the boat, I was taken down some steps and then pushed through a small opening. The kinder of the men removed the blindfold from my eyes, allowing me to see where I was. It was another dark room, only this one was damp and cold. I could feel my stomach rumbling with the swaying of the boat. He scrambled around until he found an old wool blanket.

"Here" he said, "Keep this around you. They will bring you food and fresh water every day. You are on your way to another country, so the journey will be lengthy. They will not harm you if you cooperate. You have been chosen, you are worth a lot of money to these men, so please, just do as they ask!"

With that, he opened the door, turned and looked me in the eyes once more, then disappeared through the small doorway. I was completely alone.

He was right; someone did bring food and fresh water each day. However, along with the food, I was given a pill that I was forced to swallow. It always made me drowsy, so frankly, I did not fight taking it after awhile. In fact, I looked forward to it. It helped me escape the loneliness, the confusion of the entire ordeal, and the sheer terror of what was ahead for me. What is this rubbish about me being "chosen" anyway? Chosen I was not! Stolen, abducted, taken prisoner, these words are the blunt truth, certainly not chosen.

The drugs made Gabriela go in and out of consciousness. During these times, her Papa would simply appear out of nowhere laughing and talking. She would beg and plead for him to take her home, only to wake up to the harsh reality that he was not there. It was not comforting; it felt as if he were leaving her behind time and again. When she was not sleeping, she was seasick and had a difficult time keeping her food down. It was just easier to sleep. Then one day, the ship stopped moving.

A filthily clad man came to her room shortly after the boat had stopped moving. He ordered her up the stairs, the same stairs that had brought her to this dungeon just days ago, or was it weeks? She honestly had no idea how long it had been since she had breathed the air from outside. Once she reached the deck of the boat, Gabriela could see it was not a boat she had been on, but a cargo ship—and the cargo being carried brought a horrifying shock to Gabriela.

The Search

Miguel was met at his Jeep by Papa. His eyes peered into the old Jeep, scanning carefully the front and back seats for the missing passenger, his daughter, Gabriela.

"Miguel?" Papa implored, "Where is your sister? Is she coming home later with a friend?" *A friend?* thought Miguel; they had been given strict orders from Papa about how she was to get home from work each day. Neither would dare to think of changing this commute agreement. But Miguel would gladly take any punishment his Papa considered giving him if only such a thing had happened.

"No, Papa, I don't think so; she was not in the usual place that we meet. I even went to her job. Miss Lolani said she had left early to meet me! Oh, Papa, I am sorry, I do not know where she is, or what has happened. I, too, was praying that somehow she might have gotten a ride home and was here! Papa, if she is not here, I fear for her; you know the stories of how young girls keep disappearing from Manila lately, right? What can we do? Who should we talk to? Papa, tell me what do you want me to do?"

Papa was stunned for a moment; then, when the realization of what his son was implying hit him, he fell to his knees and literally sobbed out loud, "No, God! No! Not this one, too. I cannot bear losing another child, You must help us find her and bring her back home!" Miguel looked up and saw his mother standing in the doorway of their small home. She looked down sadly for a moment, and then went back inside.

Papa took a moment to compose himself and then he ran to the house. He shouted for everyone to come to the small living room for a family meeting. He briefly explained that he and Miguel would be going back to the city to look for their sister Gabriela. He tried to reassure everyone that she would be found, although he was not convinced of this himself. Papa knew there was a chance that Gabriela had fallen into some kind of trouble and would never return home to him. His heart was breaking to pieces. He felt if he did not leave *this very second* to at least make an attempt to find her, he would have a heart attack and die.

"Everyone stay put for God's sake, and listen to your mother. I will let you know if there is any news. Onja, go get your Grandmother Nuna; tell her about Gabriela as delicately as possible and have her wait here with the family. Ask if you can borrow your friend Celina's cell phone and call your brother Pepe—tell him as well." He glanced toward his wife, gave her a confident nod, and walked toward the Jeep, calling for Miguel to hurry. Soon, they were on their way, but they did not have any idea where they were going to start the search!

Miguel knew returning to the city was something Papa had to do. He had to look for Gabriela himself, to make sure she was not still there waiting on the Luzon walkway. He also knew she had to be missing for two days before the police would do anything. The city has over nineteen million people living in the metro area. The police were not about to waste their time looking for disenchanted runaways. Unfortunately, after forty-eight hours, it was usually too late to find a missing person. Papa's silence was piercing. Miguel wanted to help his father. He longed to do something good for him, to hear him say just once, "Miguel you did great—good job, my son!" But he knew it would never happen.

Miguel continued to drive in silence until finally, they reached the downtown area where Gabriela worked. There are as many cars on the Luzon Expressway at 11:00 P.M. as there are at 11:00 A.M. It would be impossible to find anyone just driving around looking! Nevertheless, if that's what Papa wanted, that's what they would do. When they had reached the place where Gabriela was to meet him, he pulled the car over to the curb and said, "See, Papa, nothing. I was to pick her up here."

Cargo

Gabriela's eye's scanned the deck of the cargo ship and she gasped with utter shock. There, in front of her were rows of young girls, girls who looked to be her age, or even younger, perhaps. They were bound together at their ankles with a large rope; they also had their hands bound behind their backs. The girls all looked out of it, drugged. "Where had they kept them this entire time? Could they have been near me without me hearing even one of them? Why aren't I with them?" No one said a word except the men in charge who continually shouted out orders to keep moving down the walkway and off the ship. It was at that moment that I first begin to understand a little of what was happening.

All of us had been apprehended from Manila to be slaves of some kind. We were taken to another country, one far away from our families and everything familiar to us, to keep us helpless. We are all so young! There may be some as young as twelve. This is so wrong; we should be lighthearted, filled with happiness, and on our way to an afternoon with friends at the beach, not roped together like criminals. The horrifying truth is we were on our way somewhere; to only God knows where, to do whatever we are told to do. This sobering assessment struck me with overwhelming fear and anguish. I wanted to be asleep again and not to feel what I was feeling.

Once we were all off the cargo ship, there were three large buses waiting for us. The train of girls climbed aboard, the ropes still tied to their ankles. This made the process difficult and slow, but the guards did not seem to mind. The buses were old with scuffed paint, but there were some words written on the side which I struggled desperately to read. "Malaysia—*something* Malaysia." So that's where we are? The ship brought us to Malaysia? How far is that from home? I don't know for sure, but it's far enough that I know I will never be found, short of some miracle, and at this moment, I do not believe in such things. So, the fact is, I will never be found.

Once all of the girls were onboard, I was lead to the last one and told to stand in a particular spot at the very front of the bus. The girls were standing body to body, literally packed into the bus like cattle. It was hot, there did not seem to be enough air for all of us to breathe, body odor mixed with the smell of what was hauled in the bus before made me sick. I thought I might faint, which would have been a welcomed interruption to this nightmare.

I did not faint; in fact, I remained very alert and aware of my surroundings. The girl standing nearest to me was fair skinned, not Filipino. Even with matted hair, she was still quite beautiful. I decided to make an attempt to communicate with her, I leaned toward her a little then spoke softly, "Hi, you speak English? Yes?"

She glared back at me as if I was causing her some kind of pain, and then she looked away, as if to say, *just leave me alone.* I couldn't do that. I had to find out something from someone, and she was the only someone near enough for me to talk to without being heard. So I made another attempt.

"My name is Gabriela, please, tell me you understand me, and just nod your head if you do, okay?" Her face was still turned away from me, but she nodded her head, yes. "Oh, thank you," I whispered. It appeared I would have to ask all *yes* and *no* questions for her to respond to me, but that's okay, I had found my *someone.*

"Were you put on the ship in Manila?" She nodded no.

"So you were on the ship before, you come from someplace else?" Her nod said yes.

"Were you in a room on the ship with many other girls?" A nod yes. I was in a room alone, but these girls have been more than likely stacked on top of one another for days on end. Why am I treated so differently? Does it have to do with this "You are chosen" thing I keep hearing from everyone? Instantly, I felt guilty like I did at home when I got the biggest piece of mother's cake, or the ripest mango. I desperately wanted to try and even the score, level this hierarchy I had been placed in above the others, but I hadn't a clue how. I had more questions for my new silent friend, but the bus came to a stop.

I was taken off first, after being blindfolded, then led into a building of some kind. I walked upstairs—many, many stairs. I thought I could not lift my foot even one more time when, suddenly, my trek up the stairs ended. I heard my guard open a door, he shoved me through it, and then he removed my blindfold. It was a room partitioned off by curtains. They were not pretty curtain partitions like my mother had made to separate our bedroom at home, but they were there to serve a purpose. I soberly began to imagine what that purpose was. The guard pushed me forward, insisting that I keep walking to the back of the room. I tried to count the dividers as I walked past each one: eleven, twelve, thirteen…number nineteen was at the end of the tent room. My escort faced me to the right, pulled back a curtain, then spoke two words to me, "You go." Written just above the curtain was the number thirty-seven. It was written in red. He gave me a push, turned and left me there staring at my new cot.

The Others

The tiny tent room was at least not cold or damp. Gabriela walked from one side to the other and decided that her tent room was about eight feet long and close to five feet wide. She sat down on the cot and looked down at her feet. It dawned on Gabriela that she had the same clothes on that she had put on to go to work on Thursday. How many Thursdays have come and gone?

I have no idea how long it has been, but many Thursdays for sure. I wonder what my family is doing right now. Did they look for me for a week, maybe two? Are the police still trying to find me someplace in Manila?

Gabriela knew that her family must surely imagine her dead by now, and they would be right. She started to cry and said, "I am dead."

Gabriela's self-pity party was interrupted by the noise of footsteps in the tent room. A lot of footsteps! They are bringing the others to their rooms. Somehow, it helped her to know she was not alone anymore; someone was going to be just inches away from her. It made her smile and shake her head. How many times have I told my sister, Mina, "Move over, you are too close to me!"

And now, I am thrilled at the very thought of having tent mates, even if they are strangers. It is surprising what *truly being alone* does to the selfish, independent spirit in a person. I could not wait to leave my family and be on my own. Now, I would give anything for another chance to show them how much they all mean to me.

The sound of a gentle sob trickled through the curtain wall. I placed my hand on the curtain next to her so she could see its impression. I waited, hoping with all I had that she would trust my hand and reach up to meet it. I closed my eyes and changed hoping to a prayer, my first one since this entire ordeal. Then, I felt a touch ever so slight against the palm of my hand. My heart pounded within me and my eyes filled with tears of gratefulness. I had a friend.

We held our hands in place for a short moment, and then I breathed a whisper, "My name is Gabriela, do you speak English?"

A young tender voice answered, "Yes, I do. I am Kirima. I am from Bihar, India."

I wanted to know everything about her, but they continued to bring new girls in across from me and I was afraid one of the guards would hear us and punish my new friend. So I simply said, "I am so happy to be next to you, Kirima. You can talk to me anytime you're afraid, I am your friend."

I heard a sob then a whisper, "Thank you, Gabriela, so much." After that, I closed my eyes, hoping to rest, but my mind insisted on going over every detail of the day as if I were documenting it.

I was startled when someone spoke to me just outside of my tent room. It was a female voice. She said, "Hello, ya in there, Miss? I am openin' the curtain now." Then, a woman about my mother's age came over to me. She knelt down beside my cot and spoke softly to me.

She said, "My name is Darcy, but that really doesn't matter; we are numbers here anyway. You are number thirty-seven. You girls have been brought here to provide sex for all paying customers."

"Shh!" She covered my mouth as I started to scream. "Ya cannot make any noise after hours, only durin' the time customers are in the barracks, so please, let me finish, okay?" I nodded yes, but I didn't want her to finish. I wanted her to leave. I didn't want to hear another word—I just wanted to die. I was not ready to hear those words, even though I suppose I knew from the beginning I knew why I was brought here.

I moved her hand and replied, "Okay, go ahead."

Darcy continued, "I am to care for ya girls in these barracks, care in a nominal way, I assure ya. I am to check for diseases and serious illnesses that might make the payin' customers not want to come back. This is all about money, my sweet little one; these men are swine, and they are evil thugs. Please do not forget this, okay? I will be back another time, I am only allowed a few minutes with each of ya, but I am yer friend, yer Irish Guardian Angel, ya'll see."

She smiled and she was gone.

I realized after Darcy had left me I felt peaceful for the first time since I was abducted. Peaceful—how is that even possible at this moment? Yet, I am! Like the times I was frightened during a monsoon and my Grandmother, Nuna, would hold me. She made me feel peaceful, even though I was still in danger, just like my present circumstance. Darcy must remind me of her or something, because I am truly peaceful.

Gabriela closed her eyes tightly then imagined she was in her own bed with her sisters lying close beside her. She then drifted off into peaceful sleep.

A loud bell rang. It startled Gabriela and she sat up abruptly. A couple of the girls screamed out, while others began to scramble clumsily to their feet. All of them then heard their first communal orders.

"Everyone, come outside! Crawl out of your hole and stand silently." I flinched at the words *our hole*; then, immediately, I realized we were just demoted to hole-dwelling creatures! I jumped to my feet and walked—not crawled—to the front of my hole, then stood with self-imposed dignity in front of a new group of thugs.

I stood quietly, as requested. However, my mind was far from quiet. "Who are these girls, where are they from? I see that most are dark skinned like me, but there are a few others that are fair. The fair-skinned girls certainly appear more frail than the rest; perhaps, they have traveled farther. I am tempted to look at my new friend, Kirima, next to me, but dare not seem interested; they may suspect my curiosity and take her from me.

The thug in charge began to speak; he had an accent like Mr. Borislav back home. He was from Russia, I think.

"You are here because no one wants you! No one is searching for you; you should be happy you have us to take care of you. You are nothing, no one anymore, except who we say you are.

We have provided new passports that we will show you, but they will always remain with me. My name is Pavel, but you are not to speak to me at any time. Darcy, who you have met, will speak for you if necessary. Speak only to her, not each other. Punishment for speaking to each other is, well let me say: It is severe," he laughed smugly.

The group of three men, accompanied by Darcy, began walking up to each girl, looking at them with contempt; they unbuttoned some of the girls' blouses and fondled their breasts. Others were told to turn around and lift their skirts. The thugs made crude remarks then moved on to harass and humiliate each girl one by one. At least two of the girls refused to comply with their requests, and were knocked to the floor, then kicked while they were down. Cries and sounds of anguish filled the tent room. Then, lastly, it was my turn. The three men stopped and glared at me.

"And you, so you are the Princess of this group, huh?" mocked Pavel. I knew it was not a real question that he intended me to answer. I had no idea what he was referring to—*Princess?*

I thought to myself, *Well, if I were a Princess, I certainly would not be standing here with you, you moron!* My thoughts were courageous, but I felt my actions were cowardly, for I stood there without saying a word.

Then, Pavel continued his interrogation of me, "Why you, what is so great about this one, huh?" he said, turning to his spineless thug companions. They laughed rudely in my face while shrugging their shoulders, as if to say they had no idea.

"Well, join the club, fellas, because I have no idea what they're are talking about, either. I certainly do not feel special or great or any different than these other girls standing here."

22

He started to unbutton my blouse when Darcy spoke up, "Pavel, you know the orders, she is not to be touched, no one, not even you. Ya can, of course, but if *he* finds out, ya know ya are worse than dead, hum, yes?" Her words obviously angered Pavel, but had power over his quest of me. He turned away and stomped off…I am thinking to *his* hole!

His back was to me as he walked away, so I grabbed the opportunity to take a quick glance toward Kirima. She was young, but exquisite. Dark skinned, huge black eyes, thick eyebrows, and tall like me. Our eyes met for an instant and Kirima flashed a brilliant smile towards me. I branded it in my mind; her smile was my gift today. I decided at that moment that I would try to find at least one gift each day and be thankful for it, no matter how small it might be. This idea of mine would prove to be my savior in a way, giving me courage to keep going day after horrible day for the rest of my time here in the tent room.

Family

Miguel and Papa got out of the Jeep deciding they might find some sort of clue Gabriela left behind if they were on foot. It was past midnight now and the crowd in this part of the city was a very rough one. Papa was not in the least bit concerned with his own safety; however, he knew it could be dangerous, so he reminded Miguel not to wander too far from him. Neither one of them had a gun, nor could they use it if they had one. The only protection they had now were the secret prayers they both whispered. Papa's prayers were for the protection of Gabriela as well as guidance to find her. Miguel simply prayed for his sister's safety, wherever she might be. He may not have always behaved in the way he should have toward his sister Gabriela, but in the end, he would always do what he could to protect her.

"It is very late, son, we should head back home for tonight. I will contact the police tomorrow if we have not heard from your sister." Miguel agreed and they both walked to the car. On the way home, Papa slumped down in the seat; he said to wake him when they got home. He closed his eyes, but that was the extent of his rest. His mind would not allow his body respite. There is just no rest from terror once it takes hold of a mind.

Miguel looked over at his Papa. He could not help but notice that he looked much older tonight than he did just yesterday. Losing Gabriela was much worse for him. She truly was his delight. Miguel could understand that. She was not ordinary, never was, as far as Miguel could remember. It was more than just her beauty that made her special, although there was no arguing that his sister was beautiful. The quality that made her the most unique was how *she ignited energy*. It's true, he was sure he could actually feel energy coming from her at times; it seemed to fill the space all around his sister. Some said she had the ability to captivate any situation, even people. Others called it charisma, charm, personality, light, power of some kind to mesmerize. Miguel just knew it was extraordinary stuff that no one else he ever knew generated, especially him.

Back at the house, Grandmother Nuna's heart was very heavy as she thought of Gabriela's disappearance. A brief moment of joy took over her downcast spirit when she remembered what an energetic baby she had been. She truly was a delightful breath of fresh air from the moment she was born. Nuna told her often she came out of her mother's womb smiling.

Her mother would always chime in saying, "That's because of all the mischief she was already planning." Nuna never saw any of Gabriela's shenanigans as really hurtful; just plain old fun and teasing, much like her Papa.

Gabriela never fully had her mother's love. Nuna knew it was not an intentional withholding of love. Gabriela's birth was overshadowed by tragedy, which was unfortunate for them both. If her daughter-in-law would have given Gabriela a chance, the delightful new life could have been the perfect medicine to heal her broken heart. Instead, she allowed grief to overtake her chance for joy, and sadly, even after sixteen years, she allows it still.

Nuna's thoughts returned to the present crisis, the disappearance of Gabriela. There is talk of her running away to be on her own, but Nuna was certain that was not the case. "Never would Gabriela do this to her family!" she muttered under her breath. "Something has happened to our beautiful girl, I am certain." Even so, Nuna was just as confident that the strength Gabriela possessed would get her through the ordeal, no matter what it was. She was headstrong and very smart; Nuna almost felt sorry for the foolish person responsible for her disappearance. They have no idea who they are dealing with, and with that thought Nuna just had to chuckle.

Nuna was still awake when she saw the lights of Miguel's Jeep turn toward the house. Nuna always waited up for Miguel, even if it was almost 2:00 A.M. in the morning, which it now was. She yawned and got up to greet them. She was more than a little anxious to hear if there was news of her granddaughter. But the look on her son's face gave her the answer—there was no news. They walked through the door with defeat. She knew there was nothing she could say to make either one feel better. She simply gave them both an appreciative hug, told them both good night and walked slowly to the small enclosed porch. There, Nuna stretched out on the small settee, closed her eyes and fell asleep praying for Gabriela.

The following day, Papa went back to Manila with his brother, Tula, and spoke to the police, giving them all the details that he had put together about Gabriela's disappearance. He gave them names of her close friends and where she worked. He begged them to find her. He called or went by the police station everyday for a month. Finally, they told him to go home. They promised to call if there was any news. There was never a call.

In a couple of months, Gabriela's disappearance became a quiet terror instead of an outright panic for her family. Papa returned to his work on the rice farm, the girls went back to their daily chores. Mother continued with her normal canning, cooking, and shopping at the open market for fresh fruit every few days. She stopped buying mango; no one complained about not having it since that was Gabriela's favorite. People who knew whispered about the incident, but no one talked about it openly anymore. On the outside, the family looked as though they were handling things fine, but on the inside, they lived in a private pain that all families with missing children live in—the pain of not knowing.

The Deal

Lolani opened the shop door and walked in. She felt calm, almost peaceful. No one would ever threaten to take her shop away again. "The note is finally paid in full," she said as she surveyed the dress shop with a prideful eye. "It is mine—all mine. I came here from Tokyo as a young woman having nothing, and now just twenty years later, I have all I ever dreamed of. I am a very respected business woman!" She straightened up tall to boost her full five feet one inch stature, cocked her head, and said, "Indeed, Lolani, a woman who is a business owner, yes, very respected."

She removed her scarf and commenced to take inventory of the work which was completed, along with the projects that still needed attending. She admitted to being slightly behind schedule on a few special garments, but in time, she would barely even notice the absence of her young apprentice. Lolani smiled to herself, and thought, *What luck I had the day she walked through my shop door, begging for a chance to learn my trade. She was well on her way to becoming an excellent seamstress* Lolani unwillingly admitted to herself.

Gabriela's raw talent was noticed almost immediately by many of Lolani's most prestigious customers. Lolani had been envious of Gabriela's talent from the beginning, despising the fact that it took so little effort for her to do the most difficult projects. Projects that Lolani struggled a great deal with to accomplish. "I will replace her with a novice, someone to run errands and do as I say. The shop only needs one accomplished seamstress, and that is me."

I honestly do not know what they wanted with her, or why they would pay such a high price for one poor Filipino girl anyway. Her fate is not in my hands. I merely made a good business deal; she is nothing to me. What's more, her life here in Manila was not pleasurable, I am sure of that. Living with such a large family and having so little, yes, I am convinced I did her a great favor to get her out of this city. Besides, they came to me, and had already decided to take her. I just helped them a little.

Lolani remembers the day the well-dressed Caucasian man came in asking about Gabriela. "He asked me if she was my daughter—imagine the insult! I am not Filipino, I am Japanese," waving her hand and saying with contempt, "nothing alike!" He said he had a business deal to discuss with me—who wouldn't listen? He just asked to take one picture when she was not looking. He said at a later time he would call me, requesting that I send her home at a precise time of the day. These actions are not a crime—to allow a photograph to be made of my apprentice and *allow* her to leave early from work. No, not a crime at all!

Lolani's thoughts were interrupted by a police officer entering the shop. At first, fear gripped her, and then she shook it off and smugly approached the officer.

"What on earth can I do for you, officer? If it is a dress for your wife, I hate to inform you, you could not possibly afford my work." She wanted to put him in his place right away; get him out of the shop before someone saw him there. Many questions could arise from such a visitor.

"No, not looking to purchase anything, just here to ask a few questions about a girl who has gone missing. I believe she worked for you. Her name is Gabriela Mendoza.

"Well, what is there to say?" retorted Lolani. "The ungrateful girl didn't show up for work about a week ago; figured the work here was just too difficult and she just quit without telling me!"

"She didn't show up and you didn't find that a bit strange?"

"No." Lolani lied. "She was never really that reliable."

The officer wrote some things down on a pad he was holding and then turned and said. "We may be back to ask a few more questions, but I doubt it. Most of these missing teen investigations are no more than just runaway kids angry at their parents. Thanks for your time, Miss Lolani, nice shop."

Lolani shuttered and walked feebly to a chair nearby. She felt faint and knew she ought to sit down. What could she do now anyway, she contended? After sitting for a long while contemplating her choices, she said out loud. "All I can do is hope that I never hear from the police again"; and she didn't.

Hope

Once the girls were back in their tent rooms, stillness filled the barracks. Even Gabriela's spirit was somewhat broken. She knew every girl lying on her cot had the same helpless feeling as she did at that moment. *This is exactly what they want*, thought Gabriela, *to make each of us feel forgotten, abandoned by the people we love*. She knew if these criminals could succeed in this one thing, they would all die. *If we have been forgotten*, then we have nothing to hold on to, nothing to go back to, because to be forgotten is to be unloved. Why fight to go back home if there is no love there? She felt sadness began to take over her heart and mind, a foreign sensation for Gabriela, that of utter defeat.

She felt a yielding, almost submission of her heart to these discouraging thoughts. But as she lay there with fading faith, one last drop of hope began to stir inside of Gabriel's soul. Sometimes, one drop is all it takes. Soon, that single drop of hope began multiplying and turned into a giant flood of hope; and just like that, her mood changed. She sat up abruptly and whispered "I will not give up hope! I know my Papa, and he *never* gives up hope."

29

Her mind suddenly raced to one episode in particular which supported her confident attitude. Gabriela remembered when their dog, Joey, went missing. Even when he had been gone several months, Papa would still drive through the neighborhood calling his name, "Joey, Joey, come here, you ornery dog! We miss you, here boy, here." Mother would mock his effort, as would the rest of the family, except for Grandmother Nuna and me. When no one was with me, I found myself walking through our neighborhood calling his name, just in case. Then one day, Joey just showed up.

Nuna heard something scratching at the door early one morning; she thought it was the neighbor's pesky cat, as she called it. But it was Joey, dirty and terribly in need of a bath, nevertheless, it was Joey. He had found his way home. Papa had said to us many times, "When someone or something can get back home, they will, if they feel enough love, and there's never been a dog loved as much as that dog of ours." He would then wink and say, "He'll come home."

As it turned out, a neighbor who lived several miles from our home heard Papa calling Joey's name one day and out of curiously stopped him to ask who Joey was. Papa described Joey and told him a couple of funny stories about Joey's love for chasing cats. Papa always had a story to tell, Gabriela recalled fondly. Then several months later, the man saw a dog with the description of Joey chasing a cat in the alley behind his house. He placed a bowl of dog food up close to his house and, sure enough, the next day he found Joey just chomping away at the food. He coaxed him into his truck and brought him home. The story of Joey's homecoming brought fresh hope to Gabriela's heart. Surely, Papa will tell many stories about my disappearance and somehow, I, too, will find my way home…one day.

Determination

Gabriela was not the only girl thinking of her family. Kirima's thoughts were moving along the same line as her Filipino roommate.

"I must get out of here; I must find a way to get back to her." She mumbled with inner determination. Kirima's motivation was even more powerful than Gabriela's. Kirima had to get home to save her baby daughter; the daughter born to her when she was just thirteen. Kirima was just a child when her father made a deal to sell her to a man that said he needed a girl to care for his four small children. His wife had died while giving birth to the youngest of the four. He deceived Kirima's father into believing that he needed to work and earn a living for his children, and all he needed was a girl to "Watch over them," were his words.

Kirima's family was very poor. They did not have a roof over their heads, not even a small hut to live in; rather, they lived on a place on the sidewalk allocated to them. They were from a low-caste tribe in India. Many young girls of this caste were sold without even a thought that it is wrong or a violation of any sort. In fact, it was almost understood if you were a female, one day you would be sold, or end up prostituting yourself just to survive. Fact or not, Kirima never believed it would happen to her. She had lived under the false assumption that their family was different from the others. "False assumption!" she heard herself scream noiselessly. A strategy she learned while sleeping beside the man who had purchased her; purchased as if she were something to be owned. *But no one can truly be owned by another if her heart remains free*, thought Kirima.

The man may not have been able to own Kirima's spirit; however, he did have the power to take possession of her body, even if it took him longer than he bargained for. The thought of this struggle, even now, brought thoughts of victory to her mind. His first attempt at taking Kirima's innocence was not a pleasant one for either of them. She remembers sadly the day he came to get her. Her mother actually bathed Kirima herself, and then dressed her in fresh clean clothes the new owner had provided. Kirima remembered feeling happy about the new dress and the attention her mother was giving, yet feeling sad because her mother told her she was going away.

She was not quite twelve when he came for her, the day that forever changed Kirima's life. It changed her faith in love, her belief in karma, and her trust in all men. If her father loved her as he claimed, then how could he sell her? She argued, "If my mother loved me at all, why didn't she fight for me? If I was good to others, why didn't I attain goodness? If I loved my baby, how could I allow her to be ripped from my arms without dying to keep her? And if men are so superior, why do they need women?" The man—no, she corrected, "I will not call him a man, he is a *thing*, a predator of sorts, needing to devour something weaker than himself."

But he would find Kirima to be a strong and determined captive. Oh, how cunning a predator he was, luring Kirima with phony compassion. When her own father handed her over to the man that day, she was actually trembling with fear. She misunderstood his intentions as he carefully placed his hand over hers, leading her away from her family. This jester was not one of kindness; rather, it was one evil wrapped in calculated deceit. He was a hungry wolf leading a small lamb into his den. This wolf came to her night after night to satisfy his hunger. But he did not find a gentle lamb waiting for him; instead, he found an angry wildcat prepared to fight for her innocence.

Kirima fought hard. She would never forget how she kicked and scratched him until he bled, and neither would he, she thought proudly. He would never have been able to overtake her if he had not blackmailed her with the threat of going after Kirima's nine year old sister, Meena.

He said to her with contempt, "If you will not do your duty as your father agreed, then I will trade you for your younger sister. She is prettier than you anyway." Kirima could not bear the thought of her little sister being subjected to this mean-spirited man; this robber of young girls taken against their will. So, she gave into him, only to save Meena. Within a few weeks, Kirima became pregnant and he left her alone until she gave birth.

Kirima would have been more agreeable to the man when he forced himself on her after the baby if she would have known the consequences of her disobliging. But never did she imagine that he would keep her baby girl and return Kirima to her family. The memory is still excruciatingly painful. He literally dragged her by one arm for more than a mile, and threw her down at her father's feet. Then it happened, something Kirima's never dreamed could happen to any child—her own father kicked her and said, "Who is this?"

The man yelled back, "She is a devil, not a girl, give me my money back!" He wouldn't even take Meena, fearing that she would be like me. So in reality, I saved her from him after all, but in saving herself and Meena, she lost her own daughter. Kirima was certain it was a very costly sacrifice.

When Kirima's father turned his daughter away, her fate was sealed. No one would help or befriend her in anyway, lest they suffer a worse end. So, she was doomed to a life of begging and prostituting herself for a single piece of bread. She was arrested one night and placed in jail only to be raped by the guards. The next morning, one of the policemen offered to help her escape. He took her from jail and brought her straight to the thug responsible for bringing her here. Now, just two long years later, innocence is so far removed from Kirima, she can barely recall ever having it.

Kirima's thoughts were finally quieted when she heard the sweet voice coming through the curtain wall, "Hey Kirima, you awake?" It was Gabriela's voice and the sound of it was delightful.

Darcy

Darcy knew she would have hell to pay for challenging Pavel in front of the others. She had assaulted his pride. He was open and extremely proud of his spite for women. But Darcy knew the more dangerous vice that raged within Pavel was not his quick hand of assault. It was his consuming pride. Pavel's pride was the axis of his power. All the wickedness he executed evolved from his pride. He used his power like a dictator; demanding that everyone do exactly as he says, or pay the price of his fury.

Pavel has much to learn about dictatorship, Darcy thought. *There is always another evil someone scheming to take your job!*

34

Darcy believed that one day, his pride would become the death of him.

Darcy began to think of each of the young girls placed under her care. The assignment was far weightier that she could accomplish on her own. She personally had little power; she couldn't even leave the barracks without Pavel's permission. Even though she had some nursing experience, urgent situations were certain to arise that were beyond her limited training. *These girls need someone besides me!* Darcy thought. But there was no one; she was the only one who was there for them. *Tomorrow, I begin their preparation, I must teach them how to survive— survive long enough to be rescued.*

Darcy woke up early dreading her day. As she yawned and stretched, she noticed the morning sunlight beginning to beam through the windows that lined the top of the room. *Well, there is something we can be thankful for—good ventilation and light. These barracks will bring enough pain without having to mope around in the dark day after day. The fresh air will be a welcomed refresher to the lingering stench of the men's...*Darcy paused, she couldn't bring herself to actually call it what it was—she simply decided to call it a...*visit.*

Enough of the day dreaming, there was hard work to be done. She stood up, swallowed hard, and then silently knelt down on the hard floor. Her prayer was a simple one, "If ya are there sweet Mother of God, hear my prayers t'day. I know I have not been very regular at this, but it's because I've been so embarrassed about doin' some stuff that I am not proud of. I have to help some young girls get through some mighty ghastly...well to put it bluntly...crap!" Darcy stopped for a moment and wondered if she could actually say that word while praying, but after thinking about it, she figured God knew what it was, and it was definitely crap. "So, to continue, I just wanna ask for some help in doin' what I came here to do, okay? That's it for today, amen."

Darcy removed the shabby gown then slipped the cotton tunic over her head. She slipped on the worn out sneakers she had received from the Malaysian Mission and walked out into the tiny walkway through the curtained barracks. The antiquated washroom was tiny, but it had the main necessities, she supposed. She turned on the waterspout and let the cool water run through her fingers for a moment, then she splashed her face. The mirror, such as it was, reflected her unruly red hair. She pulled it back and secured it in her tattered tweed cap. "There, that will have to do!" she said in surrender. Then she walked to the bell and rang it for the first time. It was a deafening sound to Darcy's ears.

Gabriela woke to the annoying sound of a bell, "ding, ding, ding." She rubbed her eyes and for an instant, she forgot where she was. But when she heard Darcy say, "Everyone get up, step outside yez curtains and be very quiet." Darcy knew Pavel would be mad if they made noise early in the morning.

Darcy cleared the lump from her throat and began the rehearsed speech she was directed to give.

"I have a lot to tell ya girls before the day gets started. First, look above yar curtain, can ya see that number? Everything from here on out in these barracks will go accordin' to the number assigned ya. As ya may have guessed, this is a brothel, controlled by people who control all of us. I do not have power to say 'No' without losin' me own life and the same goes for you, the rest of ya. Men will pay Pavel to have sex with you, and you are to oblige these men."

Several of the girls began to sob and shake their heads. Words began to fly out of their mouths, "No, no, I won't! I'd rather die! No man will touch me. I will kill any man who tries."

Then Darcy shook her head and said, "I understand, I do, but these thugs who now control things here will punish ya so severely it will be worse than death for ya. I beg of ya to do as they ask."

"Now, the washroom is here," and she motioned behind her, "use it quickly, ther're a lot of others waitin'. There will be no privacy, so get over that quickly. Before the week is over, necessity will replace modesty. I will be by to talk to each of ya within the hour. Now, hurry, we don't have much time."

Number Thirty-Seven

Gabriela was sure she heard every word Darcy said, but her brain refused to accept the words, they just would not compute. She stood there staring at the others. Questions of rebellion rose up within. How could any human do this to another human? These are children! I am a child. How can these thugs take over our moral choices? Who gave them the power?" She was still standing in a hallway of curtains when Darcy approached her.

"Thirty-seven, I need to speak to ya privately."

We stepped inside my tent room and she told me something that overjoyed me while breaking my heart at the same time.

"Gabriela, remember when I spoke up to Pavel on your behalf yesterday? When I told him ya was not to be touched? Well, it's true. You aren't to be touched, or...violated by any man. Ya must remain a virgin because yav been chosen as one of the girls who could be selected for the harem of a man named Mr. Saku in Hong Kong."

I started to object when Darcy raised her hand to shush me and continued, "It may not sound like it, but this is considered a great honor, Gabriela. You're just a poor girl from Manila. All the other girls chosen have been purchased from very well off... guess ya could call 'em, prestigious families. Even though you're not from that world, you have a chance to be selected. *Chance,* I say because, ya still have to prove yourself worthy.

"The reason Mr. Saku approved you in the first place is because of your rare beauty. A picture was given ta him a'wile ago. He's waited all this time for ya to develop before he made his final selection. To be chosen for his harem ya must prove ya have other qualities that he finds appealing. I know this is difficult for ya to comprehend at this moment. I sympathize with the suspicions I read in your eyes, I do. I know they are tellin' ya that this is preposterous, that it can't be true, but I assure ya, it is." She finished, then took a deep breath, and motioned that it was okay for me to speak.

"Yes," I began sarcastically, "I do have just a few questions that I can think of right away...like...*harem*? Is there really such a thing still in existence? A picture of me? How? When? And who would know *him* that knows *me*? How about answer these questions because I assure you I am just getting started."

"Well," began Darcy, "Yes, harems are still in existence, Gabriela, it's just a term. But as ya probably guessed, it is simply a group of girls, or women, whose sole mission in life is ta please their male proprietor, in this case, Mr. Saku."

She explained painfully, and then preceded, "The photograph of ya? I do not have the person's name, but I do know it came from someone who knows ya well. I am not privy as to how they contacted Mr. Saku. I'm thinkin' this person had to bribe the thugs to even get him to look at it in the first place. That's all I know about these curious things, Gabriela. Think 'em over thoroughly and we can talk again later about his specific orders for while ya're here, okay? Your rice and tea is comin' in a few moments, try to relax if ya can at all, and eat somethin.'" She reached her plump arms around me with a lingering hug, and then left me alone in my tent room.

I was utterly dumbfounded by the words I just heard. I started to tremble so I carefully reached behind me to find my cot. I managed to steady myself then sat down. I had to dissect what Darcy said word by word. My brain struggled to comprehend everything; all of it together was too much for me, far too much.

"Okay," I said talking to myself, "I am being held captive in this situation; nevertheless, I am not helpless. I know there must be something I can do to alter these hideous plans. She said something about me needing to prove myself, so that means I have some time. Time is exactly what I need to work my mind around it; find a way to change this…this plan. There just has to be a way. The encouraging thing is that I have some sort of power because I need to figure out a way to use this power to help as many of these girls as I can." Her scheming was abruptly interrupted by Darcy bringing in her breakfast, rice and tea, and a much-needed reassuring smile.

I thanked Darcy for the food. I was famished. I hadn't eaten since the cargo ship. I disdainfully envisioned myself on my knees, eating without hands like an animal. "I didn't look very *chosen* at that moment, now did I, Mr. Saku?" I mocked. So all of this talk about being chosen has been true. I suppose I feel relieved in a dreadful sort of way; relieved that I do not have to prostitute myself to a lot of men, just one man...one man who must be the vilest of them all. All of these poor girls! Oh, only God knows how many more are suffering so he can be *Mr. Saku* and have a *harem!*

Courage

Most of the girls had been beaten and raped by the guards on the journey here. They also had been given drugs daily. This made it impossible for them to think clearly or react in a normal way to the information given to us by Darcy. There is no way they could service strange men all day, every day, without anesthetizing them. A simple little pill was the means of control given to them daily; an easy and guaranteed method of control. But it was also a blessing to the girls, numbing them from the full impact of this horrid violation.

Many of the girls were already living in poverty, so abducting them did not seem criminal to their captors. Some felt it a service, some sort of benevolent action on their part. After all, they were bound to end up prostituting themselves and living on the streets anyway. Why not provide a roof over their heads and food in their stomachs; a fabricated mendacity to live peacefully with whatever conscience they had left. However, there were many girls who were torn from their peaceful lives because the ringleader demanded more girls. More girls represented more money for everyone.

There also remained an outside chance of finding a one-of-a-kind beauty. Every ringleader was constantly searching for this rare find. She was the ultimate dream of all thugs working for Mr. Saku. This challenge was presented a few years ago to the head ringleaders of each zone ruled by Mr. Saku. The word quickly spread of the enormous reward offered. The money was to be distributed among the rings responsible for finding the seven girls who would make up his new harem. Saku had grown bored with his current collection and was now searching for a new group of virgins to satisfy his unrestrained cravings. The money made in brothels was fair, but the reward for discovering one of *the seven* was the real motivation that kept them going. They traveled from town to town, country to country, picking up "scrap girls," as they called them, while all along searching for "her."

The ring leader, Pavel, would never have considered searching for one of these chosen few at Miss Lolani's if it hadn't have been for an anonymous tip he received. What luck the day he followed his hunch and discovered Gabriela Mendoza. He was growing older and smuggling this particular cargo was getting more difficult. Almost every day, some new rescue organization was springing up, making problems for all of them. *Yes*! he thought, *Little Princess Gabriela just may be the one*, Pavel smirked.

Making Saku happy is also a pretty good bonus, thought Pavel. *Saku is a very powerful man and you never know what having his admiration might do for me. It could come in handy during these hard times*.

Of course, everyone knew Pavel was only powerful because of his tie with Saku. The story is they hooked up while Saku was still living in Tokyo many years ago. Saku was just a greedy, privileged kid at that time, and Pavel was working for a local drug ring. They met once at a local casino, and soon were scheming ways to make money in the prostitution business.

I guess ruthless people manage to find others just like themselves, including present company, thought Pavel, as he looked around the room. Then his eyes fell on Leonidas, "Except for him, he's different. What's he doing with us anyway?" he questioned. Pavel decided to keep a close eye on Leo, something about him made him uneasy.

Maylin

Maylin looked into the badly scratched mirror on the washroom wall. *I look old for my nineteen years*, she thought. The privacy once required of her since youth suddenly disappeared with the sound of the toilet flushing behind her. There were four girls crowded into the tiny five feet square washroom. Maylin waited for her turn to splash water on her face from the dirty sink now being used by another girl. "There is no warm water but at least it's clean," encouraged the stranger. Maylin managed a smile.

"After all, we are all in this together. I am no different than the rest, not anymore," she reminded herself.

Once the stranger was done at the sink, Maylin quickly took over her spot. *Looks like it may be a challenge each day just to wash my face*, she thought.

She glanced at a new girl entering the minuscule space already crowded; she had to squeeze by Maylin to gain control of the toilet. As awkward as it was, Maylin couldn't help but notice the exquisite beauty of this particular girl.

"From India, or perhaps Pakistan," she guessed. Maylin turned to leave just as the girl got up from the toilet causing them to bump into each other. Now, face to face, they both started to laugh.

"Well, I suppose we should at least know each other's names if we are to become this intimate," joked the beautiful stranger.

"My name is Gabriela."

Maylin smiled and slightly bowed her head, "and I, Maylin."

A couple of other girls came in crowding Maylin and Gabriela even more. Maylin wanted to stay and get to know her new acquaintance, but it felt awkward and others were waiting for their turn in the washroom, so she turned and walked out. As she left, Gabriela called after her, "Hey Maylin, what's your number? I'm thirty-seven."

"Twenty-one, I will see you tomorrow?" Maylin asked gently. Gabriela nodded yes and Maylin disappeared into her tent room.

Maylin found rice and tea waiting for her when she returned to her room. "I could eat twice this much," she muttered. "Perhaps, I will starve to death and all of this can come to an end." The thought did not sound like a bad idea to Maylin; after all, she had wanted to die for quite some time now. Maylin's life did not start out as horrible as this, though. In fact, she was very happy most of her nineteen years, seventeen of them to be exact. She remembered it perfectly because she met Nam, the son of Mrs. Woo, on her seventeenth birthday.

"It was an approved meeting, very appropriate," as Maylin's father put it. "I don't think father would approve of *this* arrangement," she flippantly said as she looked at her cot. But two years ago, I was preparing to enter into an arranged marriage, not an arranged abusive relationship. Maylin sighed and continued talking to herself about those days.

"Even before I met Nam, I was happy and hopeful that I would have a beautiful life. In fact, I found out that it was quite a miracle that I was even born." She read an article while at the University explaining that most Chinese women at the time she was conceived resorted to having a test called an ultrasound; a test which allowed them to know the sex of the child they were carrying. They had this test to guarantee them they were carrying a son, not a daughter! The article went on to explain these women felt more pressure about knowing this information because of the law the Chinese government made allowing only one child per family.

"But mother believed it was bad luck to take one's destiny into their hands, so she waited until I was born to find out she was carrying a girl, not the son they so desired," she said out loud. When Maylin asked her mother if this article told the truth, she answered, "Yes. Ultrasound was against the law, but someone truly wanting one could go underground and have it done for less than $400 U.S. dollars. But I believed it was bad luck so I waited until you were born to find out."

Maylin remembered the many times her mother said, "I was never disappointed that you were a girl, Maylin. I believe you will give me many grandsons one day!" But Maylin's father never mentioned it, not even once.

Maylin pushed the rice away angrily then said, "But that was before I was ruined and became worthless as a woman, so what does it matter if I die or not?" She buried her face into her cot and cried until she had no more tears.

Customers

Pavel was up early. Jose had brought him breakfast—his favorite, sticky rice with mango. A great start for the opening day. However, he was not relaxed. He knew it would take time to get the word out of the new brothel, and his pockets were feeling the heavy expense of this particular venture. The money he had to pay for Gabriela alone was more than he had invested in any brothel so far. "She had better not blow this for me," he muttered. He returned to his pacing while thinking, "It will be on Darcy's head if she does. Darcy knows what is expected, and she had better make sure Gabriela passes all the tests required."

There was a knock at his door; it was Jose telling him there were several customers already in the waiting room on the sixth floor. This gave Pavel relief knowing this was a great sign of things to come. They had not even opened the doors and he had already started to make money.

Jose explained to the men how much they had to pay for various services. Nothing was ever printed officially. That was too dangerous. If they should ever be raided by the police, the sixth floor was set up to look like a legitimate small business. Most of the upscale brothels set up a front of some sort to protect the customers as well as the men operating them. Small-time investment companies were the most common of the fronts. This particular farce would appear more legitimate with so many male customers visiting all hours of the day. "Yes, looking after their investments was top priority!" roared Jose.

The men paid and were told to walk up the stairs to the next floor and enter the door marked, "Supplies." Each man had been given a number representing a room; most were familiar with the routine. If a particular girl met their expectations in a special way, they could become regulars for that girl. She always kept the same number so they could find her. No names were ever used, just numbers. The girls were given strict orders to remain anonymous. They were told if any man ever obtained their name or any personal information, the police would come and take them and put them in jail. Then they would find and kill their family. But most of the girls were addicted to the drugs by now, and couldn't remember who they were, or where they came from.

The day was filled with men entering the door marked "Supplies" much to Pavel and Jose's delight. Many of the younger girls had gotten sick to their stomach and could not continue, so Jose sent some of his men to deal with them after the last of the customers had gone. The girls who had gotten sick were beaten in front of the others to show all of them what the consequences would be if they did not service the men who came to them. Gabriela was required to watch the girls being beaten so she would see how brutal the men were to them. Jose told Gabriela if she even attempted to escape, the men would beat one of the other girls until she was dead. Jose wanted to make it clear that running was not an option. He couldn't afford to lose Pavel's costly investment.

Kirima had made it through the first day much like she had for the past several months. She did what she had to do so she would not draw any attention from the guards. She wanted them to think she was just a stupid Indian girl. If they believed she was compliant, she would not become a threat, and that meant they would not check up on her as much. They would not discover she was not really taking the "pill" given to drug her each morning.

She would spit it out after they gave it to her, then she flushed it down the toilet later. She had to stay alert because Kirima had no intention of staying here long. They would discover one day that she was far from being stupid. Besides, servicing the customers was nothing to her, she wasn't even there in her mind—she was with her baby girl.

Maylin was more disturbed by the ordeal than she allowed anyone to know. She felt great humiliation after each man had left her cot. She was taking the *drug pill* every day when they brought it to her. She took it to get through the degrading acts inflicted on her, but she hated how foggy it made her feel all the time. Perhaps, soon, she could stop taking them, once she became more accustomed to the shame.

Part Two: Bonding

Assignments

Gabriela was very disturbed by the sounds coming from the others around her. The grunting of the men, the whimpers and sometimes anguishing screams from the girls. Darcy said she was coming by her tent room tonight to talk about her duties. She looked forward to it; she was not accustomed to being lazy. If her doing nothing lasted one more day she felt she would go insane. She could not even find diversion from it in her thoughts of home; they only brought sadness, then tears. Gabriela told herself she was not going to stoop to feeling helpless. She would get through this. She reminded herself that so far, she had even managed to find some sort of gift in every day. Two very special ones were her new friends, Kirima and Maylin.

It was early in the evening when Gabriela heard Darcy's voice outside her tent room, "I'm coming in, Gabriela, ya decent?" she said jokingly.

"Of course," Gabriela said in a disgusted tone while looking down at her limp, stale smelling dress. She was still wearing the exact clothes from the day she was abducted. It was the only piece of clothing she had, but at least they had not taken it from her as they had the others. The girls didn't have a single article of clothing or shoes. The guards took everything to keep them from trying to run away. If they wanted to be covered, they had to take the sheet off their bed, and after a few days, few even bothered.

Darcy pulled back the curtain and motioned for Gabriela to slide down so she could sit beside her on the cot. She patted Gabriela on the leg and began. "Now, sweet one, it's time ta talk straight with ya, yar little holiday is over," she said with a wink. "From now on, yar to get up an hour before the others to prepare their rice and tea. Ya then have ta take it to 'em. That may seem easy, but ya see, the kitchen is several floors down, so there's a whole lot of walkin' up and down the stairs, 'course you're bones are lots younger than these ol' bones of mine," she moaned then rubbed her shoulders.

"Then there's the laundry ta do as well, but that I think you're gonna learn to look forward to. The laundry is two blocks away. Now that's somethin', huh?"

Then, Gabriela leaned close to Darcy and said, "I get to leave the barracks, I get to go outside? How on earth did you manage that, Darcy?"

Darcy shook her head, "Not my idea, it's on the list, Mr. Saku's list for you, darlin'. He gets a report almost daily 'bout ya, don't ya know?"

No, actually, I didn't know, nor did I care. But I think, for the first time in my life, I will look forward to doing laundry, if it means me getting out of this place.

Darcy looked at me and studied my face before continuing, "Now, don't ya start drummin' up any wild ideas of runnin' away! You listnin? 'Cause nobody runs away from Mr. Saku and lives to tell about it, and darlin', what he would have his ornery thugs do to ya would be worse than anything ya could imagine. Them guards are evil, 'cept Leo…can't figure that one out. He can't be good though, hangin' with these ones, but still there's somethin' different 'bout him. But that don't mean ya can trust 'em now, he's still one of 'em, okay?" she said with a stern warning.

"You don't have to worry about that, Darcy," Gabriela said, "He has been with me ever since I was abducted. He probably was in on it from the beginning, now that I think about it. Who knows, he might even be the one who took my picture. He could have come into the shop or seen me waiting on the walkway and took it without me noticing. It's true, he did show me a tiny bit of kindness when he gave me a blanket on the ship, but I certainly wouldn't think him truly kind; it was simply a façade. I believe him to be more of a charlatan than someone to trust."

Darcy seemed relieved, and then she continued her list. "Ya probly won't like this one, but it's yours ta do just the same. You gotta clean the washroom ever night." I immediately felt sick. The girls using it was bad enough, but those disgusting customers used it, too.

"What's this about, Darcy? I thought I was supposed to be *chosen* or something to that nature. It sounds more like I am being conditioned to be his cleaning girl, his *feiyung*. Not that I have any say—I don't, do I?"

Darcy shook her head no.

"Right. Well, guess I better go ahead and get started. Are you showing me where things are, like the kitchen for starters? I've certainly made rice before, but at home, we always added a little coconut milk to add some sweetness, but I doubt our kitchen here will have any coconut milk!"

Darcy just had to laugh, "No, little smarty, nothin' but water. But ya'll do fine, and yes, I'm takin' ya there, let's go."

Gabriela was very eager to walk out the barrack door to see more clearly the place where she had been confined. She could barely remember walking from the bus to the building due to the drugs she was given on the cargo ship. However, she did remember it seemed like they would never get to the place they were taking her. But she figured it had to be some sort of prison—and she was right! But now, those same stairs took on a whole new meaning for her. They may have been her path to prison, but now they represented a path to freedom; freedom from the tent room, and maybe even her so-called *chosen* destiny.

The two of them started down the stairs; Darcy took hold of the railing while Gabriela followed close behind trying to count the doorways they passed on their way down the staircase. So far, they had passed four. That means the tent room barracks are at least five stories high, too far for anyone to jump without breaking a leg or an ankle—or worse. It would be very difficult to run far with a broken limb; Pavel's strategy for keeping us from running, I'm sure!

Darcy continued on past two more doors; then, as the stairs came to an end, she turned and walked through a small hallway which led to yet another door. This door had the word "Storage" painted on it. But when they walked inside the room, Gabriela could see this wasn't a storage room, but the kitchen, such as it was.

Darcy opened a small cabinet where the containers of tea and rice were kept. She pointed out the kettle, rice pot, tin cups, and bowls in the same cabinet. She sternly warned Gabriela not to allow the supply to run low.

She wanted to be notified right away if we ran low on either so she could tell Leo. He apparently is the one in charge of our delicious cuisine here. There was an old gas range with two burners, and a small sink just to the left of it. On the other side of the sink was to be my workspace; a very rusty utility table which looked like, at some point, it had wheels.

Darcy placed her hands on her hips and looked around, "Guess that's it," she mumbled to herself. She then pointed to each of them as she repeated what they were: "water...rice... tea...stove...kettle...pot...counter...cups and bowls! Okay that's it. Ya ready ta make supper?"

There was no denying it; this was definitely going to be work. It's quite a lengthy trek from the kitchen to the seventh floor, and making the same thing day and night will undoubtedly get boring, yet the thought of this assignment thrills me. It means that I get to escape the dreadful curtained rooms, along with the anguish they bring for the others.

The Chores

Soon, everyone adjusted to a daily rhythm which varied little. Darcy kept a close eye on each girl, taking care of any illness or incident that came up in the barracks. Jose kept his eye on Darcy and the customers, and a pretty little number of his choosing. Pavel kept his eye on how fat his wallet was growing and his hand on his bottle of tuba, which kept him intoxicated most of the time. Leo watched them all.

Every day before the sun came up, Gabriela awoke to Darcy complaining about her aching back and cursed cot. Within a few moments, she heard the shuffling of Darcy's feet moving toward the washroom. This was Gabriela's regular reminder that it was time to get up and get the day started for everyone. She would stop by the washroom, and then head straight for the tiny kitchen which she now thought of as her private retreat.

Being in the kitchen was the only time that Gabriela could find even a hint of peace. *It is not authentic peace, but an illusion,* she thought. "How could I ever have peace in this place?" Still, this illusion of peace managed to motivate her to arrive earlier than she needed to every day.

The truth was, merely touching the door brought calmness to her that held no explanation to Gabriela's mind. But she decided not to care if it made any sense to her. She liked what she felt. She actually heard herself softly humming a song once in awhile. She would never have imagined herself having this kind of joy again.

Serving the girls rice and tea was also something she looked forward to. She got familiar with who went with what numbers; they became faces to Gabriela. She felt compelled to pass on some act of kindness to each one of them when she could. Some mocked her efforts and called her names. Others blessed her and welcomed the gestures of kindness. "Maybe I feel guilty that I have been singled out, *chosen,* for lack of a better word. All I know is I will continue to serve them and treat them with dignity. They certainly do not deserve what is happening to them," she said with conviction.

The list of duties that Darcy had given me kept me busy in the barracks six days a week. On Sunday, Jose and Pavel actually closed the brothel so I could wash the sheets and the girls could get cleaned up. Everyone had her turn being scrubbed down by Darcy in the small wash tub. The water was always cold and there was not much soap, but it felt good to even be a little clean. I remember thinking they looked a lot like little girls getting a bath from their mother.

The first Sunday that I got to leave the barracks to do the laundry, I barely slept. Kirima and I whispered through our curtain for a short while, but she was exhausted and fell asleep. I was so excited I didn't sleep all night! Eventually, I decided to just get up and get my bath, even though I would still have to wait for the girls to leave their tent rooms to gather up their sheets to take to the laundry.

Leo and I were to leave by mid-morning so we could get all of them washed and dried then back to the barracks before too late. Pavel did not want me on the streets in the evening, said it was too dangerous. Not that he cared about me; he just cared about his investment.

Once the girls were up and about, I quickly took their sheets and placed them in the big blue laundry bag. Leo said to come down to the first floor by 10:00 A.M. and he would accompany me to the Laundromat. My arms were full but he certainly didn't offer to help. He walked toward the door and as he reached his arm out to swing it open, I noticed he had a gun on the side of his belt.

I walked through the door and as my foot stepped outside, I felt like I was on a cloud. We walked side by side. He didn't say much, but that was okay with me. Just being out in the fresh air and sunshine was heaven. I was out of the barracks for a few short hours and I didn't need conversation from anyone, least of all from one of them! I would much rather listen to the wind in the trees or rain dripping off the flowers. Everything here reminds me of my home in Manila.

We walked a couple of blocks when Leo said, "There it is," and pointed to a shabby looking building. I walked in and saw two old washing machines and one large automatic dryer. We hung our clothes on a line at home, so figuring out how to operate the dryer was going to be a new experience for me. A man looked over our bag of dirty sheets, eyed us both suspiciously, then told Leo how much it would cost. I thought Leo might help, but he just sat and read the paper the whole time. While he was reading, I gazed out the window admiring the beautiful open sky and took it as my gift for that day.

We headed back to the barracks with the clean sheets. As we got close to the door, Leo stopped abruptly and said to my utter surprise, "You're doing well, Gabriela. You are a real surprise to me. I thought you would never last one day with all the cleaning and cooking, and now this. Yes, you certainly are a huge surprise."

The clean laundry was heavy but I really didn't notice most of the way up the stairs because I was thinking so much about Leo's comment. "I am a surprise to you? You have got to be kidding, Mr. Rough-me-up one day, get-me-a-blanket the next, gun carrying, not say a word mystery man, Leo! You, Sir, are the surprise!"

When I opened the door leading into the tent room, it actually seemed sort of peaceful. The curtains to all the entrances were opened wide. As I looked at the tent room, I thought how beautiful it appeared at that moment with the last bit of sunshine beaming through the windows above. I felt a cool evening breeze on my face. It was moving the stale air out along with the offensive odors of the week. I suddenly became aware that the tent room barracks possessed a new atmosphere. I quietly placed a folded clean sheet at the end of each cot where the girls lay peacefully sleeping. *Not a bad idea*, I thought, suddenly feeling the effects of my lack of sleep from the night before. I walked quietly into my tent room then I spread the clean sheet across my cot. I started to remove my dress then vowed, "I must find a way to wash this dress next Sunday!" I stretched out on the cot, closed my eyes, and began drifting off into a peaceful sleep.

Incident

The next morning felt like it arrived sooner than usual, perhaps I just resented Sunday being over. Nevertheless, I struggled to wake up and get moving. I noticed my curtain had been pulled shut at some point in the night. Looking down at my bare body, I felt a relief. Darcy and I were the only females who were allowed clothing, but the longer I was here the less I even noticed the girls not having anything on. Most of them have just submitted to this humiliation. Admittedly, it is the lesser of degradations inflicted on them in this place.

I dressed quickly and took a quick moment in the washroom. I then headed down the stairs to begin my daily ritual. As I was measuring the rice, I heard a noise outside the door of my kitchen. "Jose is never up at this time and Pavel is still hung over," I muttered. Then I opened the door just enough to peek out. To my shock, I saw Darcy walking in from outside. She closed the door carefully while looking around cautiously. "I think she is sneaking back from somewhere. Jose would never allow her to leave the barracks without a guard with her," I thought almost out loud. As she gingerly started up the stairs, she turned around and glanced my way. Briefly, our eyes met, placing her finger to her lips to silence me. She continued her departure up the stairs.

I completed the rice and tea quite absentmindedly with thoughts of Darcy's behavior filling my mind. She obviously did not want Jose or Pavel disturbed... or aware. Which was it? Disturbed is one thing, but if it turns out to be *aware,* now, that is dangerous. I left my kitchen walking up the stairs uneasily with the rice and teapot. Both seemed heavier than usual this morning. As I entered the door to the tent room, all seemed normal. I breathed a sigh of relief and began distributing the rice and tea as usual. But I was about to discover this day was going to be far from that.

Two curtains remained closed, twelve and fourteen. I figured they had just overslept, so I called out their numbers while standing outside their curtain. "Twelve wake up! Fourteen! Hey, you two, rice and tea!" There was no answer. I sat the rice and tea down and carefully pulled the curtain of number twelve back just a little. She was not in her cot; her tent room was completely empty, even the clean folded sheet was gone. I stepped over to fourteen and when I looked in, I saw the exact same thing, no girl, and no sheet. Something was up and in my heart, I knew Darcy was part of it. I walked out into the small curtain hallway and I began to ask if anyone had seen the missing girls; no one had. I heard the barrack door open, then in walked Jose.

He yelled for everyone to get to their cots and close the curtains until he gave them permission to come out. He stomped past us, pushing a few girls to the floor that was in his way. I noticed Darcy walking toward him at the same time. They both were between me and my tent room, so I decided to step just inside the washroom, I didn't want to be in view of Jose or Darcy when this volcano erupted. The barrack door opened again. This time it was Leo with two other guards.

I could see Jose grab Darcy's arm and pull her back into the small space at the end of the barrack. "We have some serious trouble downstairs, Darcy, and you are going to tell me what you know about it…now!'

"Trouble? What ya talkin' about, Jose? What's this about?" she asked innocently.

"Don't even try to act all innocent you stupid Irish bitch, that charade is over starting now. I want some answers, or girls are gonna start dyin'. My guards informed me there were two girls missing at head count this morning, and that's just the beginning!"

He grabbed Darcy's arm and jerked it hard, then he snapped at Leo. "Leo, come get her, I want her down there to see what someone has done!" Leo quickly obeyed the irate voice while taking Darcy's arm from him. He led her through the tent rooms, then past me. She didn't look my way but kept her eyes glued to the floor. I heard Leo whisper to her, "What happened here, Darcy? Pavel has been stabbed."

When all the men were gone, I walked through the barracks informing the girls that Jose and the guards were gone. I suggested they wrap themselves in their sheet and stay in their own tent room until we heard from Darcy. I could hear the muffled sound of angry voices coming from several floors below, but I couldn't make out any of the words they were saying. I slipped quietly into my tent room and fell limp to my cot, and for the second time since my abduction, attempted praying.

"Okay, God, I do not know if I have the right to ask anything from You, but I need to, 'cause my friend Darcy is in trouble. You know what kind, and I don't, that's for sure. I am asking You that no matter what she has done to please fix it for her. She has been so good to me and these other helpless girls, surely that counts for something. I am talking to You, because this is what Grandmother Nuna always did when she didn't know what to do…and I don't. You always seem to give her an answer, so that's what I'm hoping for right now. Just take care of Darcy, don't let them kill her, okay? I promise to talk to You more, be a better person, or whatever I need to do to get You to do this one thing. I guess that's it, amen."

I remained still, hoping there really was a God and that He would come through, just this once.

Leo brought Darcy into Pavel's room. He stood beside her along with the other two guards. Jose told Leo to go quickly and lock the front door to the building, then cursed loudly saying, "There will be no flesh satisfied here today!" Leo did as Jose said and was back in the room standing next to Darcy just moments later.

Jose walked toward her, taking her arm roughly. He then dragged her toward a body lying on the floor in a large puddle of blood. It was Pavel.

"You think I know 'bout this?" Darcy questioned innocently. "Is he alive? Shouldn't we be callin' someone to help him?" she inquired earnestly.

"Does the man look like he's alive to you, idiot woman? Someone has done him in, cut him right in the gut with that broken tuba bottle," he said while pointing to a broken bottle covered with blood.

"Jose, you aren't sayin'… you're not thinkin' I did this are ya? I was upstairs with the girls; I didn't even hear anythin', did you? How could a man be stabbed with a broken liquor bottle just across the hall from ya and ya not hear nothin'?" She said with conviction.

Jose looked at her trying to decide if she was telling him the truth. He wondered how she could have done it anyway. Pavel would never have allowed her in his room, he despised overweight women, wouldn't touch 'em. Jose was in deep contemplation when one of the guards spoke up. "What about questioning those worthless girls upstairs? They probably know something."

Darcy spoke up, perhaps a little too quickly and said, "They don't know anything if I don't. They're just girls; strung out on those pills ya' give 'em ever day, leave 'em be." Her defense sounded weak and protective which made Jose even more suspicious of her involvement.

"We're going up there and find out for ourselves, they'll talk if they know anything, the boys here will see to that," he said smirking.

"Leo, you got any ideas which one of 'em it could be? Or should we just head up there and ring all their necks?"

Leo hesitated then answered, "Jose, we don't know what happened to the missing girls, or if they had anything to do with Pavel's stabbing. How could they even get in here? I doubt they had anything to do with this. We all know Pavel has made a lot

60

of enemies throughout his life. It could be any number of thugs from his past. But if you want to question the girls, we need to wean them off those pills for a few days; right now they won't make any sense."

Jose knew Leo was right. But someone had to pay for Pavel's murder and he wanted revenge right now, not later.

He took Darcy's arm and threw her to the floor, he started to kick her but stopped suddenly saying, "If I'm going to use my energy to beat her, I'm sure gonna put it to good use. Haul her upstairs guys; I want those she devils to learn a thing or two. I'm in charge now and they might as well get a lesson on how things are going to be from here on out."

The two guards picked her up and started dragging Darcy up the stairs. Jose followed close behind bellowing out curses that even made the guards uncomfortable. Leo chased after them knowing Darcy was about to get a bad beating. He knew if something happened to her, there would be no one to take care of the girls. That would mean all the money put into the scheme would have been wasted.

Once they had Darcy upstairs, Jose yelled for the girls to come out of their tent rooms. One by one, they stuck their frightened heads out.

"Get out here I said!" Then Jose and the guards began to beat Darcy. "You know something and think you can keep it from me? I don't think so," he roared. "Whatever you know, say it, where are those girls? What did you do to Pavel, wench?"

All of the girls were crying and would scream every time Darcy would. Each of them stood scared for their lives; they were at least coherent enough to know they could be next. Darcy finally stopped screaming and lay lifeless on the floor. Jose used the somberness of the moment to make a threat. "If I find out that any of you know something about all of this and don't tell me, I will do more than beat you.

"Guys, get this heap of lard out of my way," he said, stepping over Darcy. He intentionally crushed her hand with his boot to get one last bit of pain for her body to remember.

Gabriela looked up at the ceiling and said, "God, I mean it, do not let her die!"

Leonidas reached down and scooped her limp body up into his arms as if she were a small wounded bird. Gabriela suddenly became thankful for the strength and stature of Leo, which only a few moments ago, she feared. He carried Darcy to her tent room and laid her gently on the cot. He then called to me, "Gabriela, come help me. I think she is still alive."

I hurried into her room and saw Leonidas kneeling beside her, "She's pretty beaten up, but I think she'll make it. Darcy is one stubborn woman. I don't think she will die—just to spite Jose." I knew he was trying to comfort me but it wasn't working.

"She looks dead to me—you sure she's alive?" I sobbed. Leo took my hand and placed it on her chest and said, "Hold your hand here, feel that, it's faint, but still beating. She's alive, Gabriela. Now, the challenge is to keep her that way. Think you can clean her up while I go find some disinfectant of some kind? If we don't keep these wounds clean, she could get an infection and that will get her for sure."

I nodded that I would help. "What do I do?"

"Get some water from the washroom, rip up a clean sheet if you can find one, and start wiping off the blood. She's so covered in it I can't even see where it's coming from. I will plead with Jose to let me get a doctor, saying we need her to protect our operation here; he may go for it, but who knows. He's pretty outraged right now, but I'll try. If not, I will look for a street pharmacy and pick up a few things." He took me by the shoulders and shook me saying, "Gabriela, snap out of it, this is no time for you to just stand there; you want to help save her don't you?" I nodded yes, and then hurried to the washroom to gather up what I needed. Leo passed me on his way out the door and said, "Gabriela, you *can* do this, now be strong." Then he disappeared down the stairway.

More than Numbers

On my way back to Darcy, I felt a sadness come over me as I passed the empty tent rooms numbered twelve and fourteen. I suddenly realized I didn't even know their names, or bothered to hear their stories. All the while, I have been here with these girls, I have only thought of myself and my story—how I got here, and how I could survive. I walked soberly through the curtained hallway looking at the numbers above each of the rooms. I knew their faces but that was not enough for me anymore, I wanted to know them. I knew the first two stories that I longed to hear would be Maylin's and Kirima's, but right now, Darcy needed me. I thought of her lying there alone and hurried to her.

As I started wiping the blood from Darcy's body, I soon realized what bad shape she was truly in. Her face was so bruised she didn't look at all like herself. Blood was still coming from her ears and nose, which even I knew wasn't a good sign. Her right arm was now black and swollen—twice its normal size. She had cuts and deep gashes everywhere. The physical pain she went through had to have been unbearable. "Why did she do it? She could have saved herself from this beating if she would have spoken up about what she knew. Why did she just take it without defending herself? Was she part of their escape? Did she kill Pavel, or did they? He certainly deserved what he got, whoever did it!"

Darcy told me Pavel was one of the ringleaders along with Saku. He and Saku had probably made millions prostituting innocent young lives. Then I trembled as I began thinking of what the girls here had endured. What I can't figure out is how they have gotten away with it for so long. Someone has to find a way to stop this!

My objections were interrupted by Leonidas' return. He had a small bag of assorted ointments and bandages, but no doctor. "This will have to do. Jose was fearful of the police finding out… said there would be too many questions about how it happened. He's probably right, and I don't know anything about the police here in Kuala Lumpur. How is she doing?"

I was shocked by his seemingly genuine concern for her. I remembered Darcy's warning that Leo was not to be trusted, that he was after all, one of *them*. Perhaps he was just in it for the money and he didn't approve of the brutality the other guards inflicted. But approve or not, brutality does come along with the buying and selling of human beings.

Papa explained that to me when my class studied about slavery in the United States. He said, "It's just not a natural thing for one human being to try and own another." I missed him a lot right now. He would never understand this, or be able to envision his Gabriela seeing what I have seen these past few months. I left Manila a *spoiled* and *naïve* child. Today, I am vowing to never be either of them again!

Leonidas left me in charge of Darcy's care that day, saying he would check back when he could. He was very distracted, mumbling something about needing to contact Saku and helping Jose dispose of Pavel's body. I told him I would stay with her knowing all the while that I felt completely inadequate, but would try my best. I knew that I would have to leave her soon to prepare rice for the evening supper. The guards came by once more to give the girls their drugs. But we didn't see anyone else the rest of the day. When it got quiet, I slipped into the kitchen and quickly made our regular rice and tea.

When I got upstairs, instead of taking supper to each of them, I opened up my curtain and placed the food on my cot. I then went to each of the girls and told them to come quietly to my tent room at the end of the curtain hall. Within a few moments, about thirty naked girls were standing at the end of the barracks looking for their rice and tea. They started asking me questions all at the same time so I shushed them and started to talk.

"I want to answer your questions, but I really do not know much. What I do know is today has been a horrible day for our friend, Darcy. She is lying over there still unconscious. You probably know by now that number twelve and fourteen are missing…and no, I don't know anything about that! I don't have any information about customers or when you will be asked to work, or any of that. Surely, someone will be up here later to let you know."

No one spoke so I began again, "I know you only think of me as that girl who doesn't have to be with customers, who cleans and cooks and does your laundry, but I have a desire for you to know more about me than that. I want to know more about you than your number. I have some ideas about how we can do this, if you are interested."

I noticed a few nods of approval and continued. "While curfew is lax, I would like to try something very different. Tomorrow night when you come to get your rice and tea, wrap your sheet around yourself and find a place on the floor, and we can eat together and talk about my ideas then. Try to rest. I'm sure your day will be completely filled tomorrow."

Quietly they left one by one, except Maylin. She smiled and said, "We talk tonight, yes?" I nodded yes, but then she turned and left my tent room doorway. I shrugged thinking I misunderstood her request. I needed to check on Darcy anyway. I peeked in at my dear old friend and could see the bleeding had stopped but she was still unconscious. I yawned and turned to go to my own tent room, but was greeted with a delightful sight. Maylin was standing in my tent room with a sheet wrapped around her naked body complemented by a huge smile.

I had thought many times about the pretty Chinese girl that I met in the washroom several weeks back. I looked for her a few times but my life was busy with Saku's list and hers with Pavel's list. I was very excited tonight to get to know more about this timid girl. She sat cross-legged at the end of my cot with me on the other end. It reminded me of times my friends would spend the night back home in Manila. We would sleep on the back porch so we could stay up all night and talk. Once Maylin was settled, I asked her to tell me about her life before all of this.

"I am an only child. My parents, they want a son, but got a weak daughter instead."

I protested. "You certainly are not weak, Maylin," but she continued.

"I was not weak at first, but I proved to be. At first, I made them very proud. I made good grades. I made no trouble for them. My mother loved me so much. My father did not. He was not unkind, just disappointed not to have son."

I interrupted jokingly, "I can't even imagine one child—I was the youngest of *nine*. My Papa has four sons! Five, no, six daughters. But one of my sisters died. I'm sorry for interrupting you, go on."

Maylin nodded politely and continued, "Just before my seventeenth birthday, my father arranged a good marriage for me."

"He what?" I had heard rumors there were still arranged marriages in India, but I didn't think they had them in China.

"So did you know this boy? Had you ever met him before?"

"I did not know him. His father was friends with my auntie. Good Chinese parents always looking for good wife for their son. There are more boys in China. Good brides are hard to find sometimes. We married when I finished University studies. I was seventeen. I was virgin, but we finally made a baby," she giggled innocently.

I was amazed that she could blush and still possess genuine modesty in the midst of all of this. My heart was deeply touched by this rare girl. I chose her sweet tears as my gift for this day. Then Maylin got serious as she resumed her story.

"But I lost the baby after three months. We tried and I lost three more babies. Last baby was trouble for me. Doctor told us I could have no more! My husband hated me; his parents hated me more. His mother beat me every day with sticks and iron rods. They took me home to my parents, but my father said I was a disgrace to him. He locked me out of his home. I would stand at door begging him to please forgive Maylin. I could see my mother through the window. She was on her knees pleading for him to let me come in. But he has pride and could not give into her tears."

"I had nowhere to go. All my friends said I bad luck, so they must shun me." Maylin had tears running down her face. I reached over and hugged her. She was tiny and frail and in need of more nourishment. I immediately felt responsible for this, wanting to give her more food—better food. After wiping the tears from her pretty round face, she continued, "I did not know where to go. I had no money. I could have no sons. I was a worthless thing. I sleep under bridge after that, looking for food in garbage heaps at night. This was when Jose found me. He said I could work for him. He said I was still very pretty…lots of men would love me. He promised food and place to sleep. I did not know about this kind of place before. But what could I do? I had no choice."

Maylin was right, what choice did she have? I was so angry with her mother and father. Who could treat a sweet person like Maylin so badly? My mother didn't love me like the others, but she would never make me sleep on the street. Grandmother Nuna wouldn't allow it, that's for sure.

I realized at that moment how much it meant to have love in a family. Not just love from my parents, but all my bothersome brothers and sisters, my aunt and uncle Tula, and my wonderful Nuna. Papa wouldn't care if I had a son—or any children at all for that matter. And if some boy's mother beat me, well, let's just say she'd live to regret it! He would always protect me…if he could.

I enjoyed listening to Maylin's story and hearing the native accent through her tender voice. I wanted to hear more about her life, but I could tell she'd had enough for one night, and so had I. We said good night. I wanted to check on Darcy once more. So I got up and walked into her tent room. I placed my hand on her broken and bruised fingers remembering Jose's boot that did this. My friend looked bad, *but she was still alive.* Then I remembered my deal with God, and thanked Him.

Coconut Milk

Gabriela woke up thinking how bizarre yesterday had been. As she thought of Darcy's condition, she wondered what life would be like if she were no longer here. The dear lady had become a surrogate mother to the girls and to me as well. "She just has to get better! We need her."

Gabriela's stomach growled, reminding her it was time to get up and start the rice and tea for the girls. Her mind raced back to the day Darcy explained she was to prepare the rice and tea for everyone and how tiring it was to haul everything up those seven flights of stairs. She chuckled at what a sight she had become; looking more like a pack mule than a *chosen* girl of some kind. To cut down on the number of trips up and down the stairs, she decided to fasten a sling to her back that contained the cooked rice while carrying the two tea pots in her hands. "Genius!" she said, feeling quite proud of the contraption she had designed. "Well, Miss Lolani did say I had a gift for creating new fashion!"

Thinking of the rice motivated Gabriela to get up. She hurried down the stairs and opened the kitchen door, the door to her private sanctuary. Just as she started to open the cabinet to get down the rice pot, she noticed there was one lone mango lying on the counter and beside it was a bowl filled with what she thought might be coconut milk. She looked around the tiny space to see if the possessor of these delicacies was there, but she didn't see anyone. She delicately dipped her finger into the bowl then touched it to her tongue, "Ah, it *is* coconut milk – even fresh!" she delightfully said with a wide grin. The girls will have a wonderful treat this day," and as she eyed the mango, she smiled mischievously and said, "And so will I."

She steamed the rice adding the coconut milk just the way Grandmother Nuna had taught her to. When the tea was ready, she walked to the door, peeked outside to make sure no one was nearby, and then closed it quietly. She had a few extra moments so she decided to eat her special surprise. There wasn't a knife to peel it, only a large silver spoon she had for dipping the rice out of the pot. The mango was very ripe, so the spoon should work well. Then Gabriela sat down cross–legged in front of the door, closed her eyes, and put a piece of the mango into her mouth.

"UMMMMMM has there ever been anything so sweet? So delicious as this?" It was perfect, some juice ran down her chin, as she caught it with her tongue said, "Oh, no, you don't, little mango droplet, you're all mine." As Gabriela sat on the concrete floor of the kitchen, her mind wondered furiously trying to figure out just who this gift giver was? Who would do this for her? "I don't think even Darcy knows of my passion for mango." She finished half and then decided to save the rest for later.

"Where can I put this to keep the rats out of it?" She thought hard, and then remembered an empty tea tin that she had cleaned and placed in the cabinet weeks ago. She opened the cabinet and smiled, "Great, it's still here!" She placed it on the counter and removed the lid. To her surprise, lying neatly folded inside was a small piece of paper. She looked around making sure no one saw her. Then, carefully, she unfolded the paper and began to read, "I hope you enjoy the mango."

"Who? How? Why?" Her thoughts began to race wildly. "No one could have known, unless of course someone can read my mind! But no one can read minds. Oh, forget *how* they knew, *who* is it," she thought scolding herself. "If Darcy could have, she would have done something like this. But she is lying half dead upstairs. None of the girls have even been in my kitchen, so it couldn't be one of them. God knows it would never in a million years be Jose or his guards. The only person living here that it could possibly be is…Leonidas. But why would he do this for me?"

Gabriela knew the girls needed to eat so, with great effort, she made herself stop thinking of the mystery gift giver and get their breakfast upstairs. She couldn't think about this mystery anymore—at least for now.

When Gabriela entered the barracks, the girls had all finished in the washroom and they were sitting on the floor in front of her tent room adorned with their sheets. Gabriela noticed that some had them wrapped about their waists; while others wore them more like a cape. She placed the rice and tea on her cot and said, "So, now, you want to share *breakfast and supper,* do you?" They laughed and eagerly held out their dented tin cups and bowls. Gabriela enjoyed the sight, thinking for a moment they looked like children waiting for a piece of cake at a birthday party.

She smiled to herself with utter delight as she remembered the treat they had in store, the coconut milk from the mystery person that she had added to the rice. The girls were about to eat the most wonderful rice ever…her Nuna's sticky rice recipe! She filled their bowls and watched as they ate like hungry puppies while whispering quietly among themselves.

Gabriela suddenly realized there was something different about them today. She looked at them carefully when it became perfectly clear…*they were more alert than usual.*

This was the start of a brand new ritual in the barracks. Each morning and evening, they gathered in front of Gabriela's tent room to sip their tea, eat rice, and share their stories. The menu remained inadequate, but they didn't complain. They had become more than just a group of numbers; they were becoming a family.

Pavel

Jose knew he had to pull himself together and make a plan. He was, after all, the person in charge of this operation now. He knew he should get in touch with Saku soon, but first, he must attend to Pavel's body. The blistering heat was already starting to have an effect on it. By the looks of things, he had been dead for several hours. He wanted the boys to take care of it. He couldn't risk drawing attention from the local police. He walked around Pavel's room trying to imagine what could have taken place here. He quickly set aside his puzzling thoughts and returned to the present predicament; getting Pavel's body out of here without being seen.

He walked to the hallway and called anxiously, "Leo, where are you guys? Get in here! Now!" One of the guards emerged around the corner and said, "I'm the only one here, boss, you told Nathan to watch the door to the barracks and I haven't seen Leo in a while now. Whatcha need?"

"What do I need? You moron! I need your lazy carcass in here to help me with this body, but we can't do it alone. Go find one of 'em to come down here and help."

"Sure boss, but what we doin' with him? You figured that out yet?"

"Don't worry yourself 'bout that, just get one of 'em here… fast!" Jose knew he had just a few minutes to come up with a plan. He could not let things look like they were out of control. Leo might report it to Saku and he'd send in another ringleader, and he wasn't about to let that happen. This was Jose's chance to prove he could run things alone and he wasn't gonna blow it.

Leo and both guards walked through the door and stood staring at Jose. Leo spoke first. "What's your plan?"

"I think we need to wrap him up in that sheet over there," pointing to Pavel's disheveled bedding. "Let's take him out the back door and get him in Pavel's van; he can't cuss us now for drivin' it, can he?" he commented a little too enthusiastically. "Take him to that bridge about a mile from here, ya know the one?"

"The one near the casino?" Nathan asked.

"Yeah, that's it—take 'em there and when it's clear, dump it in the water. That water runs outa town, no one will know it came from here; they'll not trace it to us for sure! Even if they ID him, he's gotta record a mile long, they won't care if he's dead, just saved them a whole lot of trouble! Believe me, they don't care when one of us thugs gets it!"

"Sounds like you've got it covered, Jose," Leo congratulated. "Good job."

"Now, c'mere and help move him, he's heavy! Grab the sheet, Leo. Okay, just roll him into it nice and easy, there's already enough blood for me to deal with."

"We got 'em, now just stand at the door, Leo, make sure it's clear," ordered Nathan. Jose and the guards lugged him down the hallway, then through the back door into the alleyway where Pavel parked the van. He bought it right after they had arrived in Malaysia. Pavel always purchased some type of beat up means of transportation once he was settled into a new place. He paid cash, of course, no record leading back to him when he dumped it.

It took all three of them to lift his body into the back of the van. Jose decided at the last minute to go along and have Leo stay behind. He wanted to make sure his second-rate thugs didn't mess things up. He wanted Saku to know he could be trusted to handle whatever came up.

"Yes, mamacita, things are lookin' better all the time for your bambino, José," he said to himself quite smugly. He would never have knocked off Pavel himself, not Saku's friend. He's not that stupid! But now that he's gone, it may work out to be a good thing. Yes, a very good thing, he concluded.

As the van drove off, Leo breathed a sigh of relief, thankful that Jose had decided to leave him behind. He really needed to try and talk with Darcy as soon as she regained consciousness. He wanted to make sure no one else had seen what had happened last night.

Loss

The weeks that followed kept Gabriela extra busy. She had Mr. Saku's list of duties to complete each day as well as taking up the slack for Darcy. How Gabriela went from being one of the injured lambs to leading the flock mystified her. In fact, she thought about it every day, wondering when it was that she first began to care about the others. She knew it was more than just taking over for Darcy; she truly wanted to help the girls. She now thought of them more like sisters. Then, while cleaning the washroom one morning, the answer finally came to her. "Losing number twelve and fourteen is when things started to change in me." It was a feeling of being cheated, cheated out of knowing someone before I got the chance to.

It was the same emotion I experienced my whole life about my sister Dalisay. I lost her without ever knowing her. I was cheated out of knowing my sister in the way that others did. I hated that feeling. "Now, I have the chance to know these girls, I don't ever want to lose anyone else in my life before I know them and their stories." Gabriela felt peaceful about it now, and she knew what she needed to do about it.

She stood up from cleaning the toilet and rubbed her aching left shoulder. This is also why I lay on my cot listening to Kirima's stories through the curtain wall until late last night. She has many great stories and her delightful Indian accent...so British and all...." Gabriela teased, mocking her friend's voice; it was so entertaining. But as her thoughts turned to Kirima's story, her heart began to feel a deep sadness.

Kirima had a baby daughter that she was determined to get back. "She has a new scheme every night," laughed Gabriela.

But she was certain one day Kirima would find the right scheme and be gone. "But, when she must leave, I will know her and I will not have been cheated!"

Darcy's cuts and bruises were healing fine, but the horrible beating had broken her leg in at least two places. Kirima and Gabriela tried to help her stand for a little while each day, but the pain was excruciating it was impossible for her to walk. She was weak, but managed somehow to keep her sense of humor and was still very ornery. She even made jokes about being bedridden. She would say, "I've been on me back all the daylong like the other gurls, 'cept I'm not makin' any money!' Then she would wink at me and laugh with that rough Irish brogue of hers to reassure me that things were going to be okay. Then, one day, out of the blue, something changed. When I asked if she wanted to try and walk, she shook her head no and turned her head away from me.

"Darcy? What's the matter?" I said worried.

"Oh, sweet darlin' I just was thinkin' 'bout me life and how I may nerer get out of this bed o'mine. Makes me kinda sad... sad 'bout me life, not so much not gettin' out of me bed, but other things."

"Darcy, you are going to get better I know, and as for your life, my Papa said it doesn't matter that much about how you *start* in life, but how you *finish*. You have meant everything to me these past few months. I needed you every day, dear friend! I would have NEVER gone for this *Saku list thing* if you hadn't pushed me, and I more than likely would have taken *their pills* and given up. The girls want you back. I need you back. So stop thinking what you're thinking and get up and walk!"

"Guess ya got some of ol' Darcy's fire in ya now… ain't that somethin'? Okay, you're on. I'll do it fer ya, Gabriela! Now go get pretty Kirima and help me ta me feet."

I turned to leave when Kirima stuck her head into Darcy's room and said in a panic, "Oh, Gabriela, we've been looking for you! Number Nine, Senegal, needs some help, please come with me…now!"

"Sure, Kirima." I stood up and gave Darcy a tender hug, then said encouragingly, "We'll be back later, keep good thoughts."

As we walked, Kirima began telling about Senegal, how she had been hemorrhaging and not told anyone. "What was the girl thinking? How bad is it?"

"Bad. I'm afraid for her, Gabriela."

Gabriela's thoughts turned to the night before. "Was she at dinner last evening? I feel badly that I can't remember." I *did remember* Jose and another man going into her tent room last night pretty late, but it was not unusual to see those repulsive pigs coming out of the rooms of the younger girls at night.

Gabriela slipped into the tent room and knelt down beside her cot. She was pale as death.

"Senegal, what happened? Why are you losing so much blood?"

She struggled to explain. It sounded like she mumbled something to me about Jose cutting the baby. "Senegal, look at me," I said taking her face into my hands. "Tell me again— please, you aren't making any sense!"

She grabbed my arm and pulled me close to her face and said barely above a whisper. "He cut my baby from me!" I felt her clutched hand release my arm and she was gone.

I looked up at Kirima and started crying uncontrollably. "I can't do this, I can't! I don't know how to deal with young girls dying for no good reason! Kirima, it is too much. *Someone has to do something about stopping this brutality inflicted on these young girls!* The world outside is going on like nothing is happening! Like we're not even here! The world's eyes are blind to this injustice. Today, mothers everywhere are getting up, making food for their family, fathers are going to work, children are busy eating mango and playing with their friends, and lovers are kissing and holding each other close. People are parading into their churches and presidents are making promises to help the poor! But they don't know that a young and innocent girl just died because an evil, money-hungry man cut a baby out of her helpless body!"

Kirima knelt down beside me and said, "She is peaceful now, Gabriela, she is free…." We stayed with her a few more minutes, then wiping the tears from my eyes, I said, "Go tell the guard, *Senegal*, number nine, is dead. They now have one more dead body to take care of." Kirima gave me a lingering hug then left to find one of Jose's thugs to take care of his mess.

I ran to Darcy's room to tell her of Senegal's death. When she heard what happened to the young girl, she was outraged. I actually thought she was going to get up and find Jose herself. Jose needed to be thankful Darcy couldn't get to him. She made some comment about making it impossible for him to ever use "it" again, "that would be far worse than dyin' fer him!" she spewed. I knew exactly what she meant and I would have gladly helped her. She was still making threats against Jose when I realized in all the turmoil I had completely forgotten about making supper for the girls. I did not trust Darcy to stay put so I asked Kirima to come and sit with her until she calmed down.

I was in deep thought as I took down the pot for the rice. "I will have plenty to explain to the girls at supper this evening. Senegal will be missed. I wish I knew how to protect them better. What good am I doing them? I clean the washroom where they can't possibly ever feel clean. I cook food that is completely inadequate for their bodies. I launder sheets for their cots that only bring them humiliation! I am helpless to make anything in their lives truly better!"

The reality frustrated me. My frustration soon turned into anger…then despair. I stopped what I was doing and made a fist toward God. "What are You going to do about this?" Instantly, I heard a voice fire right back at me, "What are *you* going to do about this?" Startled, I fell to my knees on the kitchen floor, my *sanctuary*…and did the only thing I knew to do: I cried.

Explanations

Gabriela somehow felt better after the tears were released. It's as though she had a tidal wave of tears raging inside of her, constrained, dammed up, all longing to find a way to escape. Once she gave way to crying, they started flooding out uncontrollably. It took some time, but when it was all over, she was overwhelmed with peace. A peace that miraculously took the place of the anger and despair she had felt just moments ago. She knew that something had to be done to uncover all of these malicious acts, but there was rice to cook and tea to brew. That is what *she* could do right now, and so she did.

Kirima sat beside Darcy, trying her best to keep her calm. But Darcy had a lot of pent up anger inside that needed releasing. Kirima just happened to be the one that was there. It could have been anyone really. Darcy just needed to talk. She needed to tell someone her story, the story that tormented her daily.

Kirima sat astonished as Darcy began to unfold the truth she had buried deep in her burdened soul. She began the confession all the way back to her youth. Darcy told Kirima that she was married once. She had "three beautiful wee ones"; she beamed as she spoke the words to Kirima. One beautiful Saturday, Darcy's husband wanted to treat his daughters to an outing, "ta celebrate the sun shinin' day," she said smiling. "They were jest goin' to the village to buy treats. But on the road, they were overtaken by a mob of men." She later found out they were part of a gang stealing young women to sell into sex slavery. Her husband was killed trying to protect his daughters. "They we'r so young— nine, 'leven and twelve," she said with sadness.

When they broke the news to Darcy, she just went crazy. She was actually placed in a mental hospital for over a year. When she was released, she, "Went ta drinkin' like a fish to silence me demons," she confessed. One day, she was picked up by a man. He took her to a house where she was given food and a bath, and a hope that she could change, and courage to change things for others. When her demons were finally silent, she stopped drinking and stayed there to help others get the peace she had received while living there. She was so committed to helping these women and children that in time, they sent her to work for an affiliate organization. The affiliate, WACI (Women and Children International), primarily aimed to stop as much evil in as many places as they possibly could. The people there taught her to put her hatred to good use—so she did! She joined them in stopping the same type of abductions which stole her daughters and took her husband's life.

She admitted to Kirima she had been working with a secret task force for nine years trying to infiltrate into a specific gang. This gang, or ring of thugs, was involved in something called "human trafficking," a fancy word for stealing women and children and selling them to work in brothels. These brutal men were *robbing* them of their innocence and the chance to live life as God intended them to; *robbing* mothers of their children and the opportunity of watching them grow up, get married, and have grandchildren one day!

Darcy said, "Every girl me helps to free helps ta heal the pain o' losin' me own precious babes." She told Kirima she felt bad about having to pretend she was a part of this group. That she hated associating with men like Jose. But it was her part to play! She had to convince these thugs that she was one of them; she had to stay where she could do the most good. Darcy didn't mind if she died helping if it could bring a few—even one—to freedom! She considered her life nothing anyway without her family. Her only purpose in staying alive was the thought that perhaps one, or all of her girls, might still be alive somewhere. The very thought that she might be rescuing one of her own got her through beatings like the one she just endured. She felt like her suffering vindicated her in some way; vindicated her guilt for not being with them when they were attacked.

Darcy then made Kirima *swear to never tell her secret*, in exchange for helping her escape one day. This was an easy promise for Kirima to keep. Escaping from this place would be the answer to her every prayer, every minute of every day. She had to escape this hell, find her baby girl, and steal her back before her life was ruined as well.

Gabriela called to Kirima, asking her to come join them for rice and tea. Kirima called back to her. "I can't eat just now, my pretty friend; I need to be in my tent room for awhile alone."

"Is everything alright with Darcy? You seem upset."

"Oh, yes, Miss Darcy, she's…perfect. There is no way that woman is even close to dyin'; not today or any day soon. She has a promise to keep!"

Safe Place

Curfew in the barracks continued to be more lax, while guarding the door to the seventh floor became extremely tight. Jose's plan was to keep his men where they could do the most good. The gang was one guard short now that Pavel was dead. Someone obviously had to take charge and Jose knew he was the only one with enough grit and brains to do the job. As boss, he had many pressing responsibilities—much more important than guard duty.

His explanation to Leo and the guards were, "Why should we care if those stupid girls eat their rice together? What trouble can they possibly conjure up sittin' around wrapped in those ridiculous sheets all huddled up in a circle! It's not like they can think straight after we drug 'em up anyway! Just let them have their little mindless tea party for now."

No one was going to argue with him about that. Fewer restrictions meant less trouble for them. So, the girls continued meeting every morning and evening eating their rice and sharing their stories. Gabriela took advantage of this time to began privately building them up, helping them gain some self-respect; convincing them they were still valuable, even if evil men treated them like they were disposable.

Gabriela told them, "No one can truly rob us of our dignity if we believe we have value! *It is what we think about ourselves, not what others think, which instills our true value.* I refuse to believe that I am what they tell me I am! Stop feeling defined by what others force you to do. Define who you are by your own independent choices—even if they are few."

She went on to talk about the way they should treat each other. "Be kind. Don't just think about how hard this is on you. Start caring about what your sister is going through as well. If you hear her crying in her tent room at night, then offer to sit with her in the dark for a while until her sadness leaves. Clean up after yourself in the washroom. Leave it in good condition for the next girl. If someone is sick, let me or Darcy or Kirima know. We cannot let something happen again like it did to Senegal; check on each other. Even when Darcy returns to her duty of caring for us, don't stop caring about each other!"

What Gabriela said that day was not spoken in vain. Little by little, the girls began to change. Many even chose to stop taking the "mellow pill," even though it meant they were more aware of the revolting men they were forced to service each day. Being aware of it mattered less and less to them. They now had something to look forward to at the end of each day, stories of hope and how it *might be one day*, when they were free. Gabriela had no idea if any of them would live long enough to experience freedom outside of these rooms. That is why she continued insisting they must all find freedom within.

She pleaded with them. "Find your inner safe place and go there in the midst of cruelty, viciousness, heartlessness, nastiness, malice, and brutality. Find that place and you will discover you *can* get through these times."

Sadly, the abuses endured here were not the only exploitations the girls needed to be freed from. Most shared stories of ill treatment since they were quite young. One girl was in a brothel before coming here where she was kept in a cage let out only to service customers. She actually felt blessed to be chosen by Jose to come here. Her story broke Gabriela's heart. But there was also Kiana, whose own aunt came offering to rescue her at age nine from her abusive parents. However, she herself owned a brothel; she was nothing more than a female pimp, who immediately started advertising her niece as an available young virgin. She took Kiana knowing what a valuable piece of merchandise she was, an innocent child. She was not being rescued as the sweet girl supposed, but being sold, because somewhere in this wretched world, there were men willing to pay enormous sums of money to sexually abuse a very young virgin girl.

As Kiana sat in the circle and told her story, Gabriela's heart no longer was breaking, but rather getting enraged. There were many more that had been prisoners in sex slavery who were even younger than Kiana! Their lives were threatened with butcher knives to be cut to pieces and eaten by dogs. They feared for their very lives, they were held captive! The pimp would dress the girls in seductive clothes applying makeup to their innocent young faces. She imagined them looking like a child playing dress up in their mother's things. But they never were allowed to *just* be children. Gabriela's heart changed from *just feeling sorry* for girls like Kiana, to being utterly outraged! She stood up and bravely declared, "One day, I will leave these barracks, and somehow I will do everything in my power to abolish these horrific acts inflicted upon girls like my sisters."

The girls all came from different backgrounds, yet they were connected in a unique way. They were like a family who were linked together because they shared the same last name: *Abducted.* This common last name certified that the girls were a family. They would always possess this particular bond regardless of what their own personal stories were. Their first name was their past, their age, their color, and cultural accent—they each had their own. But their new last name would forever define these girls as family—*abducted.*

Reality

Gabriela had no idea why she was compelled to take on this campaign of freedom for the girls. She never thought of herself as brave or noble by any means. In fact, she had been very much the opposite of this in her past. She was the baby of the family, very spoiled, demanding her own way. She really did not care what her siblings wanted or needed, she was only interested in attaining her own dreams. Dreams of getting out of the ghetto! She was driven to have an abundance of material things. Things she had been denied because she was a Mendoza child. Now, none of those things mattered. She was sad to think they ever did.

When she heard the stories of genuine suffering like so many of these young girls endured, she realized how very blessed she was. She lived in a house with a roof and a floor. She had clean water and food at every meal. She had brothers and sisters who loved her, and parents to protect her. Gabriela's life, in a brief moment, had been reduced to doing whatever it took to survive. When one's survival is threatened, one becomes keenly aware of what is most important, and it certainly is not material things. This proof was all around them even though they were completely cut off from the world.

The obsession of wanting more and more money was what kept the girls here in bondage to Jose, Saku, and all the others on the payroll. Money and things must not be the basis of happiness. If it were, then why would Mr. Saku destroy thousands of lives just to get more of it? Darcy said Saku had inherited millions. Apparently, millions were not enough; it just drove him to want even more. This was proof that no amount of money, in itself, could bring happiness and peace. Gabriela had already learned through this wrenching experience that loving people—not things—was the most important treasure in life to seek; the treasure of loving and being loved.

The thought of *love* suddenly brought to mind this so-called destiny of hers. She was the girl *chosen* to be part of a harem, but in reality, it was just a gloried term for sex slave. She folded her hands and placed them over her heart and said, "I must put to death my childhood dream of finding passionate love with a man who adores me. I will never know this kind of love."

She began to think of it more honestly than she had allowed herself up until today. I will be living in a harem with six other girls all competing for one man's love. This is a man who has already proven by reputation that he has no love to give. A man that thinks so little of love that he has girls chosen for him by men like Jose. Girls that he fully intends to discard one day when he grows bored with them!

"Gabriela!" she scolded herself out loud, "Get your foolish heart in line with the reality of your future. There will be no adoring love with living happily-ever-after with Prince Charming. How could there be?"

Her thoughts were interrupted by Darcy calling to her. "Time for me walk, Gabriela? I need to start gettin' stronger ya know. Can't stay in me bed much longer, my mind is just too busy! I need ta be takin' care of you now sweet babe. Darcy promised to watch o're ya so I best be at it soon."

"Anytime you are ready, Darcy, I will gladly hand it all back over to you. Kirima has been a big help as well. She is not one bit intimidated by the guards. The only tears she sheds is over missing her little baby girl. You know, Darcy, she lies in bed night after night making a plan to run away. I fear one day she is going to try something and get caught. I could not bear anything happening to her."

"Oh, I wouldn't worry 'bout Kirima, Gabriela dear, she is smart and wants to stay alive for her babe. I'm thinkin' she will get outa here...one day in time."

"I pray you are right, Darcy."

"Now, will ya really, Gabriela?"

"Will I what?"

"Will ya pray—ya said ya pray—will ya do that?"

"I haven't had much faith in praying these past few months, but I did pray for you, and I have to admit, you are still here. I did make a promise of sorts, so yes, I will pray that Kirima does get out of here to find her baby girl."

"Well, your prayers must be powerful ones, based on me still livin' in all, I'll just bet she does."

"Now, do you want to walk, or are you just gonna sit here blabbing all day?'

"Let's go," replied Darcy, getting up and taking Gabriela's arm. She had learned to love this girl so much. She was proud of how far she had come and knew it would not be long until Mr. Saku would be sending for her. This made Darcy a bit sad, but also knew Gabriela's destiny was out of her hands.

Leonidas

Leo took his turn guarding the seventh floor barrack door. He watched as the customers came in and out all day; some of these girls serviced as many as forty men a day. Jose was putting a lot of cash in his pockets while sending Saku plenty as well. Leo and the other guards only got a small amount of the money compared to them, but Leo could care less right now about that. He was here to watch Gabriela and make sure she would get to Saku exactly as she was supposed to. "Untouched with no blemish," were his instructions for this rare beauty. Leo had just spoken to him yesterday. The other six had been chosen and have started the second part of their training. Saku wanted Leo to hurry and get Gabriela ready to move from Malaysia.

Leonidas knew she had a few more things to complete before she was ready to leave here, and it had nothing to do with Saku.

"Hey, Leonidas," Gabriela said, interrupting his thoughts of her.

"Ah, hi…hello. Ah…you about ready to go to the laundry for the week?" He spoke nervously, taken back by her sudden appearance. It made him uncomfortable to have her show up while he was thinking about her. Like she could read his mind or something!

"I will be ready at our regular time today. Do you think it will rain…again?'

"Pretty certain it will rain, but maybe we can go early and beat it. Could you manage that?"

"Sure, I have to serve their morning rice and tea first, but then I will take their sheets from them right after and then we can leave."

"I'll be waiting here."

"Okay, see you in about an hour then."

Gabriela wondered if Leo was okay, he seemed preoccupied, not himself. But she decided not to give it much thought. He never was much of a conversationalist anyway. Maybe he would surprise her today and actually say something instead of reading the paper the entire time she was doing the laundry. The girls finished their Sunday rice and tea then handed over their sheets to be washed for the week. Gabriela noticed the sheets were getting pretty worn, but they still did the job. "They covered up…what they were supposed to," she said to herself, uncomfortable with all that meant.

Leonidas was quiet on the walk there as usual, but once she had the sheets in the washing machines, he started to talk to her.

"So, this circle you have with the girls. What do you talk about exactly?"

"Everyone just talks about whatever is on their minds, nothing really important." She lied.

"You honestly think I'm gonna believe that? They wrap up in sheets, sit for an hour or more on a hard floor to talk about nothin' really important? Just how stupid do you think I am? No, don't answer that!" he said almost jokingly. Gabriela was shocked that he had a moment of almost acting normal.

"Well, if you must know…I have encouraged them to get to know one another, become caring and kind and a whole bunch of other things that I know you are just gonna make fun of and tease about, but I don't care what you think! It has helped all of us to change how we're living together. We aren't making plans to escape or anything—don't worry!" she added flippantly.

"So, you think by getting them to do this sharing and caring thing it is going to help them in some way? Locked up in here? Having to do what they have to do every day, several times a day? That…THAT is your way of trying to help them?"

"Well, it's a lot better than what they were doing before, Mr. High and Mighty!"

"Look, if these girls got out of here tomorrow, I mean if I unlocked the door to the seventh floor and set them free, within two days they'd be prostituting themselves for a piece of bread and a place to sleep. Or come back here begging me to let them back in!"

"You…you…pig! There is no way that would happen! You are wrong, I don't believe it!"

"Well, I hate to burst your little fantasy bubble, but they would. I have statistics to prove I am right."

"Oh, really? I'm listening!"

"They have been labeled whores! The cities, or people in them, are not going to overlook that important detail and welcome them with open arms. Who do you think is going to hire these girls who can do nothing but turn tricks? Most of them are addicted to drugs by the time the gang gets done with them. These girls are doomed to sell themselves in the outside world for survival. What do you think they will do for food, Gabriela? Do you think they know any other way to provide for themselves other than selling their body for sex? They risk their lives attempting to escape from pimps in order to be on their own, but end up doing the exact same thing a few hours later because they are hungry and have no money and no place to go. Tell me, how do you expect these little speeches of yours to put food in their stomach? And when they have babies, and they will out on their own, how are they going to feed them? They do not know how to do anything else! It's like I said, they would be back in a couple of days begging us to let them back if they ever did escape."

Gabriela was quiet for a long while and then began to address what Leonidas had said about the girls. "Wow, that is hard to hear, Leonidas, but what you said makes sense. Now, I understand their dilemma. For them to make it on their own without any training or work skills would truly be impossible."

Gabriela didn't want to talk much after this conversation with Leonidas; she had too much on her mind. She really wanted to help them, not just give haughty speeches. She was determined to find a way for them to take care of themselves if they ever did get out of this place.

They walked home with the clean sheets side by side, uncomfortable with the silence. Just as they got close to their building, Leo spoke up. "Look, Gabriela, don't let the truth about the girls get to you. It is what it is. But as bad as you think I am, I really am not the brute Jose is. If any of these girls could escape, I wouldn't want them on the streets begging or prostituting. So, keep up your meetings and if you come up with any ideas to change things, I'll do what I can. But it has to be without Jose knowing. This has to be something we keep quiet about. If Jose knew I offered you help, I would be the next body dumped in the river with Pavel. I have a job to do and that's to get you safe to Saku.

"Why, Leo, that's...kind of you, truly! I have no idea right now, but I will be thinking about it. I would *never* tell Jose anything about anyone. That's a promise I can make to you on my mother's Bible.

Leonidas smiled and said, "Your mother has a Bible? I'd never guess that."

His comment was confusing, but so was Leonidas. He was a man with many discrepancies.

Circle School

That night, Gabriela lay awake for hours on her cot thinking of what to do, but nothing seemed possible. There was no way to help the girls become something they were not. They needed to learn how to do something besides turn tricks, or that's what they would do when, or if, they were ever free. She tossed and tumbled so much that she woke Kirima up.

"Gabriela, what's the matter with you? Every time I fall asleep, you turn over and kick the curtain or your cot squeaks and I wake up."

"I am sorry, Kirima. I do have a lot on my mind tonight. I will try to be still so at least one of us can get some rest."

"Whatever it is, Gabriela, I am sure when you go to your kitchen tomorrow, you will find the answer. You always come up with great plans when you are there. Now, close your eyes. Good night."

"You are right, I will think about it while I am cooking the rice in my little sanctuary. Good night to you my friend—my sister."

The next morning, Gabriela could not wait to get to the kitchen and find the peace that seemed to fill the room. She felt a new sense of hope like she would find an answer soon. It was in this little kitchen that she heard a voice inside asking the sobering question, "What are *you* going to do about it?"

As she stood thinking about the question, she said, "*What* can I do? Well, I have an hour in the morning with them and one at night. I should use it in a way to help them even more." She hated to admit it, but Leo was right. Feeling peaceful and having self-respect is great, but it won't fill an empty stomach. Then, it became perfectly clear to her what she needed to do. She needed to teach them skills to survive. Some simple things, but with Leonidas' help, along with Kirima and Maylin, it just might be possible!

She could not wait to get breakfast over with so she could get Kirima, Maylin, and Darcy in her tent room. She needed their support to make this happen. There seemed to be urgency in her spirit.

When all four were neatly tucked into her room, she started unfolding the plan. "Okay, I know this is going to sound a bit outrageous, so please let me finish before you walk out on me. It has come to my attention that almost everyone here has no way of taking care of themselves or their family," she looked straight at Kirima, and then continued. "If they ever got a chance to be free, the only training most of the girls have is prostitution. Well,

I want us to change that!" She saw the objections on their faces but said, "Wait—hear me out. I know there are some important things that we each have that we could teach the others. Maylin, you have studied at the university. You certainly can teach them to read and write. Kirima you can teach them how to defend themselves if they get attacked. We all know you know how to kick and scratch!" They all laughed, remembering how, as a young girl, she fought off a grown man for weeks and weeks to protect herself from him. Darcy, you must know how to cook, don't you? I mean the basic stuff, how to make potato soup, beans, cheap and easy—teach them how to make it. You could teach them about eating right with fresh fruit so plentiful here; they should eat it often if they get away from here. You know what to teach them, right?"

"And you master teacher, what will you teach them?" Maylin inquired.

"Master I am not, let me assure you. But I do have an amazing hand stitch that any seamstress would love to have done on fine garments. I can teach that!"

"Everything sounds great, but how are you going to teach them to sew without sewing needles and everything else we need?' asked Kirima."

"We will have to do it with very little supplies, but I do have someone I think will help me get some supplies. Maylin, what do you absolutely need to teach them to read and write?"

"A small chalkboard, chalk, a book or two?"

"How 'bout one book?" questioned Darcy

"You have one?" Maylin asked doubtingly.

"As a matter o' fact I do. I have the best Book in the world. I have me very own Bible. It's worn out and half gone, but 'tis a book at least!"

"How about you Kirima, what do you need?"

"I just need *myself* to teach them about how to hit and kick in all the right places to hurt 'em and keep them off!" Everyone had a good laugh just imagining that sight.

"I can teach 'em…I remember a few things 'bout cookin'," Darcy admitted proudly.

"Okay, then, Maylin and I are the only ones who need something to be able to teach our class, is that right? Maylin, you probably will only get one small chalkboard.

"I will work on getting the things we need. Until then, start working on your daily teaching plan, we need to help these girls know how to be something besides prostitutes." Everyone agreed and left the tent room with their own new sense of purpose.

The following day, Gabriela saw Leonidas and told him she had a plan and asked if he was still willing to help. "If I can, as long as I don't get caught, what do you need?"

"I need three or four sewing needles, several spools of thread, and a couple extra bed sheets. A small chalkboard and as much chalk as you can get. How does that sound?"

"I'll see what I can do. As long as you don't plan on using one of those needles on me, I think I can smuggle them in to you later this week. Hopefully, that's all, right?"

"Well, now that you asked, I sure would love another mango!" She said with a big smile.

He shrugged his shoulders and said, "Mango? I don't know what you are referring to."

Confession

The plan for the circle school gave new energy to Darcy. Her recovery had been slow until Gabriela gave her this amazing new way she could help again. The WACI had slowed down their attempts to get the girls out because of Pavel's death. They couldn't risk blowing Darcy's cover. The leaders knew they must get her out before the sex ring leaders discovered she was working undercover. Darcy was vital to the WACI's work. But they also knew these men would torture her in ways that no human should suffer to get her to talk. The organization could not take any chance of being compromised, so they stopped all rescues at that location until the turmoil of Pavel's death calmed down. Teaching the girls in the circle school was something that Darcy could do to help the girls in the meantime.

There was nothing she could do about the ordeal that occurred with Pavel anyway. It was out of her hands from the beginning. Pavel's irrepressible lust for young girls and cravings for more money is what really killed him—that and sacrificial love.

No one knew, not even Darcy, that number twelve and fourteen were sisters. The girls were walking home from attending a movie one evening when two men from the gang overtook them. They were pretty Caucasian girls whose father was in the military. He was stationed just outside of Manila. The older of the two, number twelve, was fifteen years old and her baby sister was eleven.

Twelve was determined to protect her sister at all cost from the moment they arrived. When Pavel sent customers to the young girl, they would end up frustrated and demanded their money back. Twelve would try to stop them from complaining to

Pavel by offering herself to them. She was willing to do *anything* if they wouldn't complain about her baby sister to Pavel again. But over time, the complaints were far too many for Pavel to overlook. He was not about to put up with a non-productive girl and decided to put an end to this standoff himself.

One night very late, he and Nathan slipped into the barracks to get both twelve and fourteen. Twelve had pretty much confirmed to Pavel that she was protecting the young number fourteen. He was sure they knew each other and suspected they were sisters.

He was right about his suspicions and decided he could use it to his advantage. Pavel and Nathan got the girls out of the barracks without waking the others. Once they got them in Pavel's room, they gagged them and tied them up. Pavel gave Nathan a bottle of tuba and told him he wouldn't need him for the rest of the night. Nathan loved tuba more than anything and was appeased with his reward.

Pavel tormented the girls with graphic explanations as to what was about to take place. After drinking a full bottle of tuba, he untied the older sister, and then began to rape her while making the younger watch. He made threats like, "I'll show you what it costs to refuse a customer! This is how it's done, you little worthless dog! You better watch 'cause you're next!"

The young sister kicked and squirmed trying to set herself free. She watched as this monster raped her sister making her cry. She had never witnessed such brutality. Finally, after being violated over and over, number twelve fainted and Pavel dropped her to the floor.

"Well, now, little missy, it's your turn, and I promise you won't be a virgin when I'm done with you tonight!" he laughed with demonic scorn. The frail young girl became hysterical as

Pavel began his vile speech at what he was about to do to her. Just as he was about to take her, he felt something hit his skull. The muffled screams of the young girl had caused her older sister to regain consciousness. In an attempt to save her baby sister, she grabbed one of Pavel's tuba bottles and smacked him over the head with it. It broke the bottle but only stunned Pavel. When he realized what number twelve had done to him, he went after her with full intentions of killing her. In great fury, Pavel reached out and grabbed her. The broken tuba bottle was still in her hand, she defensively plunged the sharp glass deep into his gut as hard as she could. Pavel dropped to the floor with blood gushing from the wound. She untied her sister and consoled her for a brief moment. Realizing they were in serious trouble, she instructed her sister to stay put while she ran upstairs to get Darcy.

Darcy will never forget the panic-stricken look on the girl's face when she woke her that night. With a frightened whisper, she began to explain, "Darcy, please come, I think I've killed Pavel."

Darcy quickly rushed down the stairs to confirm what twelve had confessed to her. Darcy took a quick look at Pavel's body in the pool of blood, knowing right away he was dead or close to it. Surmising the situation, Darcy was aware she had to get the girls out as quickly as possible. She walked over to Pavel's desk and picked up his phone to dial a number she had memorized. It was to be used only in matters of impending, severe danger. She spoke quietly to someone on the other end, then hung the phone up and turned to check on number fourteen.

"It's going to be okay, I have a friend on his way here right now. You need to go with him and do exactly as he tells you. You can trust him; I swear to you, he will not harm you. He is coming here to rescue you from Jose and the others." She looked around the room to find something of Pavel's to cover the girls. She found a jacket and shirt and told them to quickly put them on. She then walked silently to Pavel's door; she needed to make certain all the commotion had not disturbed Leo or the other guards. After seeing the hallway was clear, she motioned for the girls to come. Darcy unbolted the large front door and hurriedly walked the two frightened children out. The sun was coming up and she knew they needed to hurry.

A man in a hooded sweatshirt walked toward them. Darcy hastily hugged each of the girls and said, "You'll be a'right now, just go!" and they disappeared into the early morning light with the hooded stranger.

As Darcy crept quietly back inside, she heard the sound of a door opening. When she glanced at it, she saw that it was Gabriela already in the kitchen preparing the morning rice. Darcy stared at her momentarily then placed her finger to her lips requesting her silence, then continued up the stairs. She knew it would not be long before Pavel's body was discovered and she would somehow be held responsible.

She will be forever grateful for Leo's intervention that morning when he suggested it may have nothing to do with the girls. The beating she took was hard, but with each blow, she felt a supernatural strength enabling her to take it. Darcy knew the strength came partially from her own guilt being atoned for not being with her family the day they were attacked. But there was also something divine giving her strength as well. She knew in her heart that it was God.

Now, she was getting another chance to help the girls here in the barracks in a different way, thanks to Gabriela's plan for the circle school. She couldn't wait for her part to begin.

Circle School Begins

Leonidas was able to find the few supplies that Gabriela requested and plans were made to start classes the next morning. Gabriela asked her little teaching staff to conduct a meeting in Darcy's tent room to divide the girls into smaller circles so they could work more easily with them. They would learn one skill in the morning and be taught another in the evening. After a couple of months, they would change to the other teachers, to be taught the other two skills. All the girls would have four months to master all four. These skills would enable them to make it on their own if they ever were set free.

Finally, it was time to begin classes! There was a new atmosphere of hope in the tent room barracks. The morning began early with the usual rice and tea, and then they broke into their smaller circles for class.

A few in Maylin's group could read a little, but most of them could not read or write at all. She used the small chalkboard to teach the very basics to them, then relied on the ones who could read to help her teach the others. They had only one book to practice their reading. Each girl would take her turn then pass it on to the next girl throughout the day. The girls were smart and picked it up rather quickly. They were like starving little birds just waiting for their next meal of knowledge. It was very satisfying to Maylin.

Kirima was rejuvenated teaching the girls how to defend themselves. She showed them where men were most vulnerable and how to kick and make it count. She also taught them how to slug a female pimp to knock her down. Kirima warned them it was not always safe to use force. Sometimes, they would have to resort to plain old trickery on their attackers. Kirima had also mastered this skill quite well. Like how to act insane, or deathly ill. Crazy or sick girls could not be sold to pimps or brothel owners, so they would pass them up for someone else.

Darcy had fun pretending to make delicious meals without having even one real ingredient to work with. The girls seem to catch on fairly well, considering they were cooking in an imaginary kitchen with pretend food. But she had them memorize easy recipes explaining in the strictest detail the way it would look and taste when it was fully cooked.

Gabriela's class was a bit more difficult, so a few dropped out. She ripped up the sheets to make smaller pieces of cloth so they could practice the delicate stitching Gabriela had learned from Miss Lolani. A few showed real promise. She had dreams that one day maybe they would be hired by an alteration shop or maybe even work as an apprentice in a dress shop like she had. She was thrilled that the skills she loved so much might one day be of real use in someone's life. It didn't look like she would ever get to use them again herself. Becoming a professional seamstress was another one of her dreams that had died with all the rest. She now had dreams and they were not all centered on her.

Everyone worked hard and within just weeks, the four teachers were bursting with pride over the progress of their students. Things in general were tolerable in the tent barracks for now.

One

One morning, Darcy came to Gabriela with a worried look and asked if she would meet her down in the little kitchen to speak privately with her. Gabriela said yes and began to try to figure out what could possibly have Darcy so worked up. The circle school had just one month remaining before the classes were completed; she hoped Jose had not decided to reinforce curfew.

Darcy walked with Gabriela downstairs to the little kitchen, carefully closing the door behind them.

"Sweet one, I need ta speak with ya 'bout somethin' very serious, and I need ya ta just listen 'til I'm all the way through before ya say a word."

"Okay Darcy, but hurry up, you are starting to really scare me. What's going on?"

"There's so much 'ya don't know 'bout me, sweet girl. Well, there's just no other way ta say it, but ta just say it right out. I am here workin' in the barracks for an organization who works ta free abducted girls from men like Pavel and Jose. Since Pavel's death, there has been a leak of some kind that I'm here. They want ta get me out before I'm discovered. I don't want ta leave, but they're makin' me. They say it's for the protection of the whole underground movement. They cannot afford it ta be compromised."

"Darcy, whoa…that is a lot! It kind of sounds like something out of a movie—you're telling me you are part of an underground? You?"

"As crazy as it sounds, yeah! I've been involved for a number of years; I have had the privilege of helpin' free hundreds of girls like these ones here."

"Well, Darcy, I don't want you to go, of course. I will miss you. I need you, I love you! I can't even imagine the barracks without you! But I want you safe, and for this underground thing to continue doing what it can to help."

"Thank you sweet babe for understandin', but there's more. When they come for me, I can take one of ya girls with me. Ya can come with me, Gabriela—ya can be set free. Ya wouldn't have ta go ta Saku! Eventually, you would get back to ya family," she said sweetly. "But ya must decide before tonight."

Gabriela stood in her sanctuary kitchen flooded with waves of joy at the thought of leaving the tent room barracks...tonight! Then another larger wave, one of guilt came flooding over her. How could she just choose herself over all the others? What is the right answer?

"You decide, Darcy, I can't. You tell me who should go. How do I pick just one, when I could be *one* of the ones?"

"I don't know how ta pick, sweet one, that's why I'm givin' ya that job. If you want ta come, no one can know, we just have ta leave when I say. We have it worked out for tonight when Nathan is on guard. I have a whole bottle of tuba to give him; he'll be passed out cold and we will walk right by him. But you can't say good bye—to anyone! Ya hearin' me?"

"I am—I'm just not sure I can make that kind of decision!"

"I'll leave ya be, but just so ya know, in time, the organization *will try* to save the rest of the gurls. I can't promise when that will be, or if it will be soon enough for some of 'em. I'm pretty certain a couple have HIV/AIDS. Damn this place!"

"Alright, Darcy, I'll let you know…soon."

Darcy left Gabriela standing with the most important decision of her life. Perhaps, the most important decision of someone else's life, too. She thought about being free, going back home and getting to be with everyone again. But in the middle of her thoughts, she began to feel like the people who were once her family now felt more like strangers to her. She corrected her thoughts, "No, I've become the stranger! I am not the same Gabriela I was just a few short months ago. Going home, being free is what I want, but… it's really not time for me to go yet."

"Well, that's half the decision! If not me, then *who* should it be? Why did Darcy leave this decision up to me? They all need to be free from this place—all—not just *one* of them." She saw their faces in her mind staring at her one by one. She began to cry, she could not bear to leave any of them behind. But as she looked at each girl's face her mind stopped and focused on one. The one who had planned on leaving here from the moment she arrived—Kirima! She had a baby girl she must get to and rescue. To choose Kirima over the others would really be like rescuing two instead of one. She's the one. Kirima's dream of being free is going to happen! Gabriela's heart felt relieved and confident that she had made the best decision possible. She looked around her sanctuary, sighed deeply, and then said out loud, "Kirima's freedom is my treasure for today—a treasure that I will forever hold, but it is a treasure that I must also give up. She opened the door and walked slowly up the stairs; she knew in just a few hours two of her dearest companions would be gone forever from her life.

Gabriela knew she needed to talk with Kirima as soon as possible. She should speak with Darcy to hear the escape plan.

"It will be wonderful to give her this news, I know this in my mind, but my heart is so heavy I can barely hold back the tears," she spoke under her breath. She waited until she knew Kirima was alone then asked her to come into her tent room.

"Gabriela, you know Jose will kill me if he catches me here with you in the middle of the day. What is so important it can't wait until later?'

"Well, you might want to sit down on my cot to hear what I've got to say."

"Gabriela, if you don't tell me right now…"

"Alright, but promise you will not say one thing…not one…. you hear me?"

"Okay, okay I promise, what is it?"

"Darcy is in some underground thing and…"

"Oh, Gabriela, I already knew that! Is that what you've got to tell me? Goodness you had me scared half outa my mind!"

"No, I told you NOT to say a word, now listen…she is in the underground and for a reason that I am not going to get into right now…they are removing her from here tonight! No, not a word out of you yet! Because they are getting her out, they have told her she can take *one* of the girls with her. That girl is *you* Kirima—you! You are leaving this place in just a few hours!"

"Gabriela, this better not be some wild dream I'm having. It's not, is it? I'm awake, I'm here with you, and not on my cot dreaming this is happening? It's real, right?"

"It *is* real, my pretty Indian sister, it is definitely real. Now, you do need to finish up your day, like nothing is any different. You don't want to tip Jose or the others off. You can't risk anyone suspecting that there's something going on. When you can, get to Darcy. She will tell you what to do, I don't know that part."

"Okay, I will get back to *that*," she said, pointing over to her side of the curtain, "in just a minute. But right now I've got to say goodbye to my family." Taking Gabriela by the shoulders, Kirima stared deep into her dark brown eyes, and with tears running down her face she said, "I've got to say goodbye to my sister, my beautiful, smart, and compassionate sister. I love you Gabriela, and I will love you forever. I promise I will find my baby girl, and now, thanks to you, I can take care of her on my own. I hold you in my heart." And with that said, she hugged her and walked to her side of the curtain.

Gabriela needed a few minutes to collect her composure before telling Darcy of the choice she had made. She was sure it was the right one, but it hurt to let her go. Just knowing that Kirima was going to get the chance to find her baby girl made the hurt bearable. In a few brief hours, Gabriela would not have anyone beside her or across from her in the tent room. It will be strange—it will be lonely.

Before going down to prepare rice and tea for the evening, Gabriela stopped in and told Darcy her choice. Darcy was proud of Gabriela for the sacrificial love she was showing Kirima. Darcy knew the beautiful Filipino girl who was *chosen* was just about ready to leave here herself. Gabriela had no idea she had just completed the last assignment on Saku's list. She would also soon be on her way from here…on her way to Hong Kong.

Kirima could not swallow one bite of rice at supper. Her heart was beating so hard you could see it beating through her sheet dress. Darcy looked at her with caution a couple of times, reminding her to settle down. They could let no one suspect that anything was brewing. Kirima made it through class with the girls then went straight to her tent room to try and compose herself while waiting for the lazy sun to go down on this day. *This is the longest five hours in history*, Kirima thought. She paced back and forth. She lay down on her cot; she got up and repeated the same ritual over and over again while trying to contain the excited squeals which wanted to fill the entire room with her happiness.

But finally, it was time to leave; her freedom hour had arrived. Just as she was about to walk to Darcy's tent room, Gabriela stepped just inside of Kirima's room. She was completely naked. Kirima had never seen Gabriela without her dress on, in fact no one in the tent room barracks ever had.

Gabriela had her dress draped over her arm when she walked in. She reached out her arm to Kirima and said, "Here, this is for you. You can't be running through the streets of Kuala Lumpur with that ridiculous sheet wrapped around you. I'll take it; you put my dress on, quickly." Gabriela and Kirima knew that the underground would give her a dress soon, but it was a token of love that Gabriela was offering to her friend that night. It was the only thing she had left from home; it was all she had to give her. Kirima changed quickly into the tattered dress her dear friend gave her. The two friends held each other for a long tender moment and then Kirima was gone.

Gabriela walked back into her tent room once she knew Darcy and Kirima had left. She could not manage another painful goodbye. She slipped quietly back clutching tightly to Kirima's sheet. "I'll figure out how to wear this thing with style," she said trying to be funny in hopes to lift her spirit. It didn't work...at all. She started crying again burying her face into the cot. She gave herself permission to grieve just one more time over the loss of her dear friends. After a short time, she fell asleep and dreamed of a better life for all of them.

Gabriela woke up late. She jumped to her feet knowing she could not allow anything to appear different today. Darcy and Kirima needed time to get as far away as they could from here before the gang started looking for them. Gabriela hurried to the kitchen to start the morning rice and tea. Making sure that things looked normal was something she had to do, no matter how much her heart was breaking inside. Her inner strength obliged her need and she walked calmly up the stairs to face the inevitable scene at hand.

The girls were already waiting in their circles when she got to the tent room barrack.

"It's about time, Cinderella!" Maylin teased. "We're all starving, and don't forget we need dresses for the ball." Everyone laughed even though each probably didn't understand her joke.

She is in wonderful spirits today, thought Gabriela. *I am sorry it won't last long; Jose is sure to notice Kirima is missing within the first hour they are open for business.*

"Where's your dress anyway?" asked number nineteen. "You want to look like us, right?"

"Well, sure I do, besides it was past time to retire that worn out dress of mine anyway," she answered convincingly. But the two teachers' absence was sure to come up any moment, and she had to act as bewildered as the others for her own safety. Then it came, her first lie about the escape.

"Where's Kirima?" Maylin asked.

"Yeah, where is she? Darcy's not here either. Have you seen them today, Gabriela?" inquired one of Darcy's students.

"No, I went to the kitchen as usual. I haven't had time to even notice, but you're right, they should be here by now. Look in Kirima's tent room; see if she is still sleeping. Darcy could be downstairs in a meeting, who knows about her." Gabriela thought she sounded pretty convincing.

"She's not in here!" shouted one of the girls.

"Well, maybe she's with Darcy, I have no idea where they are," Gabriela said truthfully, because she really did not know *exactly where* they were. "But, let's go ahead and get started with class. Maylin and I will divide their students between us and do the best we can today. Maybe we'll be back to normal tonight." She lied, knowing full well nothing would ever be normal again in the barracks for any of them.

The girls seemed to let go. Maylin, though suspicious, went along with Gabriela's plan for now; besides, she had other things on her mind today. It would not be long before she had to share her own secret with Gabriela, but it wouldn't be today, not yet.

After class, the girls went back to their tent rooms waiting for Jose to send up their first clients of the day. Gabriela also began cleaning the washroom and even gave her kitchen a thorough going over just to keep her busy until the rumbling volcano blew. It was just about time for it to erupt and she wanted to be out of Jose's way when the hot lava began to spew. She even felt sorry for Nathan; Jose may kill the poor man who couldn't refuse the bottle of tuba. Wow, come to think of it, this is the second time getting drunk on tuba led to catastrophes lately. One would think this to be a lesson for all of them! Jose drinks, but not like Pavel and Nathan. Her thoughts were interrupted by Jose's angry growl down the stairs.

"Gabriela! Get up here...now!"

She took a deep breath, and then hurried up the stairs to pretend not to know anything…about anything.

"So, where is your little Indian whore friend and that good for nothing Darcy? Don't tell me you don't know either! They don't do a thing without you knowin' about it. So come on, give it up! Where are they?"

"Jose, all I know is they were not here this morning at our circle. I just figured they were with you! Or doing something for the guards or…I don't know. I certainly wasn't worried about them." Gabriela told the truth about that, she was not worried in the least about them! She was relieved they pulled it off and were free. However, she was a little worried about herself and the others right now. Jose was sure to take out his vengeance on the girls and make it as tough on her as he could without jeopardizing Saku's precious cargo.

"You really expect me to believe this *estiércol?*" I could only imagine what that word meant in English. It was a word I never heard my grandmother Nuna use, that's for sure.

"You know where they are and I intend on getting it out of you one way or another, even if you are Saku's Princess slut! Leo, get her downstairs to my office. She's gonna talk before the morning is over!"

Leo walked toward Gabriela, taking her by the arm. He escorted her down the stairs while anxiously planning his speech with each step. This all took him by surprise and the timing was not good, either. He really needed Darcy's help in completing Saku's list for Gabriela. But she's obviously gone, so where to go from here is what he needed to be thinking about. He would have about one minute to stop Gabriela from getting beaten to death once they got to Jose's room.

Once they were all inside, Jose started the interrogation. He got in her face demanding she talk. She just stood without saying anything in her defense, which made Jose even more irate. He'd had about enough of her insubordination.

"You insult me by not even answering my questions? Are you loco? You think you are so special? I can ruin your pretty little face with just one slash of my knife! You have received special treatment your whole life for your beauty, no?"

"That's enough," Leo interrupted.

Jose looked at Leo then he spit in Gabriela's face. "Leo, you might need to leave for a few minutes. You don't need to witness what I'm about to do to this pompous little brat!

Leo paused, then started in bravely to state his objection. "Jose, you know I can't do that. I work for Saku, not you. My job is to get this...what did you call her, pompous brat?—to Saku, *untouched, without blemish*, you know the terms as well as I do. I work for him same as you. Now I'm gonna do my job, Jose, that's all. I'm not here to defend this girl! You know I have no choice when it comes to carrying out one of Saku's orders. Even if I wanted to let you rough her up, or even kill her for that matter, Saku would have both of our heads once he discovered it. And you know he would, he has his ways. I say she's not worth it! She's certainly not worth losing my life over; how 'bout yours? Leave her alone. What could she know about this anyway? You think she's smart enough to break those two outa here? You give her that much credit, huh? I say, replace Kirima with a new girl, fresh meat always brings a higher price. Darcy hasn't been worth keeping around since her beating. I think your concern should be your own head right now. Jose, you need to bring in more money to prove you a good a ring leader. You can do whatever you want with the others, they are not my concern. But you will have to kill me before you get to her. You ready to do that, Jose? You want to answer to Saku's wrath?"

Jose knew Leo was right. His anger and frustration had muddled his thoughts. He needed to get a hold of himself and prove he could run this operation. His objective was to make a lot of money for himself and Saku. That meant his energy needed to be used in finding a new girl and getting her to work as soon as possible. He would request a couple of new guards today; ones that wouldn't be controlled by tuba.

Leo was relieved that Jose bought into his argument and allowed Gabriela to go back upstairs unharmed. He certainly had not planned on getting this involved with things here. He wanted to get back to what he came to do; see that Gabriela completed Saku's list and made it through the next part of her training—that's all. Saku called yesterday wanting her in Hong Kong soon.

She and I will be leaving here within the month anyway, I just need to stay focused on that, and that's all, he lectured to himself. The last thing I need is to care about this girl. She was chosen for Saku's harem and as long as she completes his list, then she will become number seven. Nothing must interfere with that!

Once Gabriela was safe upstairs, she started thinking about what a close call she just had. Jose was planning on beating the information out of her, that's for sure! Knowing the kind of brutal man he was made her tremble. *He will stop at nothing to find out what I know*, she thought to herself.

Gabriela was very thankful for Leonidas' rescue. But the things he said about her belonging to Saku slapped her back into reality pretty quickly. "Perhaps, I fooled myself into believing I, too, would escape and not have to go through with the dreaded act of belonging to Saku's harem. I know my time to leave must be getting close, Darcy warned me it was."

"I have a mission I hope to accomplish with the girls before that happens, though. Maylin and I have one month left to complete the circle school. I hope I have time to at least finish what we started, and completing the girl's training will remind me that I did something good, at least once in my life! Then whatever I must do, I will."

Surprises

The month passed quickly and soon the last of the classes in circle school were completed. Maylin worked hard alongside Gabriela. She was thankful that Maylin didn't complain about having to make up for Darcy and Kirima's absence. Not only did she refuse to complain, she even showed up early everyday smiling and full of energy. Gabriela certainly had noticed a positive change in Maylin. "She said she needed to speak to me today after class, I'll ask her then." Her thoughts were interrupted by the sound of Maylin's voice.

"Gabriela, may I speak with you...alone?"

"Well, sure, let's go into my tent room. What's on your mind, Maylin, you okay?" She certainly looked okay; in fact, Gabriela thought she looked better than when they had met several months ago.

"I am very good. I have two secrets to tell you, my friend."

"Well, I hope these secrets of yours won't cause Jose to get upset again. I have had enough of his anger for a while. So will they upset him?"

"Oh, no, he is very well informed—at least of one. He is happy man about it."

"Really? Jose happy? Go on."

"I have a customer that is regular. He has come only to my cot since he first came to barracks. He comes to me two maybe three times a week since then."

"Maylin, several of the girls have regular customers, and of course that makes Jose happy. Happy customers keep coming back, and don't they have to pay more if they request one particular girl?"

"Yes, they pay more. My regular customer is a good man from the U.S."

"Maylin, why would you think your man from the U.S. is good?"

"He is not like the others who come to me. He is not rough and talk dirty and ask me to do bad things. Many times, we just sit on my cot and talk whole time. No tricks, not even a little, just talking. He is older man with no family. I think he is just lonely."

"That, I have to admit he is very different. He pays just to sit and talk? So what do you talk about?"

"He is businessman. I do not know some things he says, but I just listen and laugh when he makes funny joke. That was at first, but now we talk more serious. He says I am most special girl; that I am very pretty and smart…."

"Well, then, he is a smart man, you are those things and so much more, Maylin."

"He surprised me a few months ago when he asked me if I would like him to try to buy me."

"Maylin, I do not think Jose will sell you, not without a lot… and I mean *a lot* of money."

"He told me I was worth whatever it cost; he does not want to leave Malaysia without me. He said he must take me with him."

"So did he ask Jose yet?'

"He talked to him yesterday. Jose said he was crazy to want to buy me, that I was getting old, that he should get new young girl. Jose offered to find him one with new cargo coming."

"My man said he could not afford a young girl; that he hoped to get bargain since I had been violated so many times."

"So, he fooled Jose into thinking he was just hoping for a bargain? Wow, that's pretty good."

"Yes, he is a very smart businessman," she laughed. "Jose made him pay too much just the same, but my man knew he would, he just did not want Jose to know how much he wanted me; just bargain, that's all he wanted Jose to know."

"Well, I do have to admit, that's very wise of him. If Jose had any idea that he really cared about you, he would never let him have you. Jose does not want anyone happy but himself."

"He made deal yesterday and paid money, I am leaving today."

"Maylin, are you sure Jose is going to let you leave? I mean, Jose is really not a man to be trusted when it comes to deals… especially if he already has the money."

"That is the good part, he wants me to leave. He wants my cot for new girls coming in soon. He thinks he stole the money from my man, because he was going to get rid of me anyway.

He does not want to lose the deal. He told me I better not mess it up for him that I was to go with customer without any trouble. We both fool Jose!"

"That is such good news, my dear friend. So, you are leaving today? So soon?"

"Yes, he is waiting downstairs for me now. I told him I must say goodbye to my sister. So, I came here to say goodbye, Gabriela. I had to tell you of my secret. I wanted you to know that I am happy about being sold. I did not want you to be sad over me."

"Maylin, thank you for telling me and I am happy for you. I promise not to be sad, okay? Now, go, he's waiting."

"I will go but I have one more secret, the best of all. Maylin has baby growing inside, see?" She pulled the sheet tight across her stomach, revealing a pretty large bump protruding from her stomach. "My baby comes in three more months I think. It kicks me every day to say, 'I'm still here, don't worry.' It's already good baby to help me not to worry!"

"Maylin, you're pregnant? I thought they said you couldn't have any more children? I mean that's the whole reason Nam and his mother kicked you out in the first place, right?"

"Yes, but they not know everything…my man says this will be miracle love baby. He said Nam not love Maylin, that's why babies died. My man says he knows this baby will not die, because he loves Maylin and baby feels it!"

"I am overwhelmed and filled with joy over your secrets. I love you, sweet girl. I am so happy that you are getting another chance, that this man, Mr. U.S. man, found you, because you *are* special. I knew that from the start." She hugged Maylin and kissed her stomach. She looked her dear friend in the eyes then said, "Hey, let's get you out of here! I will walk you down the stairs. I want to see this good man of yours."

They walked arm in arm down the stairs, and just as Maylin left, she turned to Gabriela and whispered, "And I think it's a boy!" then she laughed a bit mischievously.

Gabriela watched the older man gently take Maylin's arm. He opened the door and they walked out together…and just like that, she was free.

Gabriela walked to her kitchen to have a few moments before going back to the others. She sat down on the floor. Memories of Darcy, Kirima, and Maylin flooded her thoughts. She remembered the day she bumped into Maylin in the washroom and how exquisite she thought the shy Chinese girl was. She smiled thinking of Kirima's hand touching hers through the curtain their first night in the barracks. And, of course, the day that Darcy brought her here into this scanty little kitchen and told her about the list and being chosen.

Her thoughts immediately imagined each of them being free. She thought of Darcy working for the rescue of more girls through the underground organization, of Kirima reuniting with her baby girl, and Maylin finding love while working in a brothel. What joy it gave her to know all four of them were free and fulfilling the destiny *chosen* for each of them. Now, it was time for hers to begin.

Part Three: The Harem

Leaving

Gabriela woke up feeling lonely and was anxious to get to the kitchen and start rice and tea for the girls. Staying busy was the only thing that made the loneliness bearable. She walked down the stairs and opened the kitchen door. As she opened the cabinet door, she noticed a package sitting on the counter. A note was attached with her name written on it. Gabriela opened the note and read, "You will need this today, hope it fits."

She opened the package and inside was a dress. It was pretty, but simple. It was blue with puff sleeves. She was dazed, completely bewildered. "How could anyone know about me wanting a dress almost exactly like *this*?" She held it up forming it to her body. It looked like it would fit perfectly. She clung to it for a moment, delighted with the thought of wearing it, then the sobering words on the note sank in, she was leaving here…*today!*

She heard a knock on the door; it was Leonidas. "See you found the dress. You think it will fit? We need to prepare to leave shortly. Is an hour enough time for you to...ah, say your goodbyes?"

"Sure, I will tell the girls with the morning rice and tea. Do you know who is going to prepare it for them after I leave?"

"Jose has someone lined up for the job, not sure who. But, they'll be fed, Gabriela; they're not your worry anymore. So, I'll see you down here in an hour? Dressed and ready to leave?"

"Yes, I will be ready." She thought, at times this man seemed almost kind. But Darcy reminded her often not to forget, *Leo was one of them.* "I know he is, but there is something different about him and I intend on finding out what that is."

Leonidas has been with me from the beginning. I recall his behavior being different from the others in that first room I woke up in. He stared at me pleadingly to eat and do what the guards told me to do. Then on the cargo ship, once again he seemed to care, at least a little as he gave me a blanket to keep me warm. He held on to me when I was weak and could barely stand on my own while waiting on the deck of the ship. Here in the barracks he defended me against Jose, and helped me by getting supplies for the circle school. I think perhaps it was he who left the mango, but I can't be sure of that.

On the other hand, I cannot dismiss the fact that he is part of this ring of thugs; and also working for the *master* of the entire operation, Mr. Saku. He has been unfriendly, cold, distant and unkind most of the time we have spent together. "Yes, Leonidas, you certainly are a mystery!"

Gabriela decided not to put the dress on just yet; she wanted to say goodbye to the girls wearing the sheet which bound them together in a way that no one else could understand. The sheet itself was nothing but a piece of dingy cotton cloth wrapped around their bodies which, if seen by others, would think it pretty silly. But not to them, the sheet covering was a constant reminder that they were valuable; that it was up to them to choose everyday to believe that, regardless of how others treated them. It appeared to be a simple sheet, but it really was a symbol of value.

As Gabriela looked at them huddled on the floor laughing and talking with each other, she thought to herself, "They all look like beautiful Roman princesses." This is the memory she chose to keep of them in her mind forever. This is the last treasure she would take from the tent room barracks, her *beautiful Roman princess sisters*.

She watched them from the barrack doors a moment longer, then gently closed the door, passed the guard for the last time and walked slowly down the stairs to the destiny chosen for her.

The Journey

Leonidas was quiet as they walked to a taxi waiting for them in front of the building known to Gabriela as *The Tent Room Barracks*. Leo opened the door for her and she slipped into the back seat of the taxi; he then walked around to the other side. Just as he started to get in, Jose yelled from the front door, "Ya leavin' without telling me? Don't I at least deserve a goodbye?" I peeked out the window and saw him walking toward us.

"Oh, great, just what I didn't need!" Leonidas said under his breath.

"I want you to tell Saku something for me when you see him," Jose began.

"What's that, Jose?"

"Well, let him know that I have things here under control. I expect to be making more money for him…within the week. I have a load of fresh new cargo coming on Friday…Saturday at the latest."

"Just call him, Jose; you tell him, I've got to get Gabriela to Hong Kong and prepared for her introduction to him, lots to do yet. I wouldn't want to forget to give your message to him."

"You know he doesn't take my calls like he does yours. He doesn't think of me like Pavel just yet, but he'll soon see, I'm as good as he ever was—maybe better!"

"Don't sweat it, Jose, just show him, he's a hard one to convince until there's proof, ya know. Doesn't care about talk… just wants to see the money!" Leo tried to tease.

"Okay, if you think that's the best way, I'll show him! Not worried 'bout that."

"Jose, I've got to leave, we have a flight to catch out of here, so good luck with your plans and reaching Saku." Leonidas jumped into the car and said, "Please, let's go!" he ordered the driver.

On the way to the airport, Leonidas reached into a bag and pulled out some leather slippers and said, "Remove those worn sandals, and slip these on, okay? It's time for you to start looking presentable."

"Alright, and by the way, thanks for the dress, it's nice."

"I'm glad you like it."

He acted irritated, almost nervous. I thought perhaps he was stressed about the conversation he had been forced to have with

Jose. It was obvious he was trying to get out of saying goodbye for some reason, but couldn't manage to pull it off. So I just kept quiet even though I wanted to talk and ask a hundred questions like, "Where are we going exactly? Am I meeting Saku this week, this month? When? Will I meet the other six girls soon? And the one troubling me more than any other…who are you, anyway?"

We arrived at the airport and Leonidas paid the driver. He grabbed one small leather bag and walked around to open my door. When I stepped on the curb, I stumbled slightly and Leonidas instantly grabbed me. He acted genuinely scared. "Gabriela, you okay? You feel alright?"

"I just slipped, sorry. It's probably the new shoes. I'm okay, truly. Maybe, I should be scared or afraid, but I'm not for some reason. Just a few months ago, I would have been terrified of meeting such a man as Saku. Hearing of the pain and suffering the other girls had to endure throughout their young lives, I think meeting Mr. Saku is not so horrible that I cannot bear it."

"You have certainly grown up a lot in these months."

"Now that you mention it, just how long have I been away from my home?"

"Gabriela, we need to get in the airport and check in for our flight. We can discuss all of this later. Traffic and the delay with Jose's conversation made us later than I wanted, come now, hurry along, will you? Now, just in case you have some ridiculous idea of running away, or telling security that you are being abducted, you better listen to what I am going to tell you, Gabriela! If you should try to run, Saku will find you and you will end up in some God-forsaken rat hole. But the worst part is he will have your mother and father killed. You haven't really seen what these men are capable of, so please I beg of you, just cooperate. Understand that your life as Gabriela Mendoza is dead."

He handed me a passport and said, "You are now Ella Muñoz."

I looked at my new passport. The name Ella Muñoz appeared alongside a photo that I don't remember being taken. Where did they get this picture of me? Should I cry out for security to help me? Would my family really be harmed if I tried to escape? Knowing what I knew about the men who worked for Saku, I took the threat seriously and decided not to say a word.

We managed to get checked into our flight to Hong Kong and got through security just fine. We walked past a food court as I looked longingly at common sandwiches and pastries which now looked like fine delicacies. Leonidas, seeing my hunger, stopped and offered, "I think it's time for you to end your rice and tea diet 'Ella.' Come here. What would you like first?"

I felt like a child getting dessert for the first time. My mouth watered and desired everything. What would I choose? "How about a lumpia with some sweet dipping sauce? I also would love to have that mango, yes, that one in the back." I chose carefully, like Grandmother Nuna taught me. "I'll take some cold bottled water, that's all, thank you."

Leo paid and we walked to our gate and sat down. I inhaled the lumpia. It wasn't nearly as good as the ones my mother made, but it was heaven to my taste buds today. They had provided a plastic knife to peel the mango. I looked at Leo and said, "I could have used this a few months ago!" He acted completely confused by my joke, like he didn't have a clue what I was referring to. I just shrugged and continued to prepare my treat. I peeled and sliced it ever so gently, then picking up a piece I put it into my mouth, then closed my eyes while savoring its sweet juice and rare texture. Oh, how I had missed eating this wonderful fruit. Then I remembered where I was and once again began questioning Leonidas about how long I had been missing.

"Do you really want to know? I can't imagine it making things any better, probably will only make it worse, Gabriela, I mean Ella."

"I want to know, Leonidas, how long?"

"Eleven months."

"What? How long?" I began to instantly recall the long days and nights spent in the barracks and the journey on the cargo ship…how could it be possible that I have been away that long?

"I said eleven months. I told you it would not make things better, didn't I?"

"Things cannot be worse because I know! Things are worse because I am here with you and not there with my family! Almost an entire year, which means I am almost eighteen."

"I know how old you are, Miss Ella. I think I must know everything about you by now. No more questions that will not make things better. We need to go, they are boarding our flight."

I wrapped up the mango and walked with Leonidas onto an airplane which would take me even further away from my family. How could anyone follow the trail from Manila, to Malaysia, to Hong Kong? There are millions of people in all of these places. I am just one young girl who used to be Gabriela Mendoza, going to a world I know nothing about to become someone I will never be. To belong to a man I will always despise. This…is what I was *chosen* for, this is my destiny?

Arrival

When the plane landed in Hong Kong, Gabriela was frightened, anxious and had to admit feeling a bit of excitement. This was a city she had only heard about, never dreaming she would ever see with her own eyes. Why had this man gone to such great lengths to bring her here? There must be many beautiful women right here in Hong Kong, certainly more suitable for what he had in mind. Perhaps, one day, she would come to understand it, but right now, she remained completely confused.

After landing safely at the Hong Kong International Airport, Leonidas told Gabriela to stay near him and not say anything when they went through customs. "Remember the warning I gave you leaving Malaysia, your parents will be killed I assure you, if you even bat an eyelash in the wrong direction. You understand?"

"Yes, I get it! I will not make a move unless you tell me to."

They got through customs without any trouble; they looked at Leonidas' passport and smiled, welcomed him home and barely looked my way. Walking through the terminal, Leonidas reached into his pocket and pulled out a cell phone. He touched the front of the screen, and then placed it to his ear. "Hey, it's us. We've landed. Can you head this way to pick us up? Which car will it be? Okay, we'll see you in about forty minutes." He turned to me and said "Well, Miss Muñoz, you are about to enter your next phase of preparation and hear about your new list. I don't think you'll mind this one as much as the list Darcy gave you in the barracks."

"Ah, another list, huh? What is it with Mr. Saku and his lists? I am thrilled just at the thought of it!" she said mockingly.

"Well, like it or not, there is a list waiting for you to complete. You will hear about it tomorrow after you get some rest; and Gabriela, someone will be bringing *you* breakfast."

They walked out through the airport doors and once outside on the curb, Leo turned and waved to a big black car. It was shiny and looked brand new. The driver stopped and got out. "Welcome home, Sir, you just have that small bag?" He looked me over quickly and said, "I think you are right about this one, Mr. Saku will be very pleased after Lyn get's done with her!"

"Lyn?" I asked looking at Leonidas. He nodded yes.

"Sir?" I asked sarcastically.

He rolled his eyes and said, "Just get in, okay?"

As we drove toward our destination, I tried to read as many signs as I could. We were on Lantau Highway for several minutes when we passed Discovery Bay. It was lovely with the moon light shimmering on the water. We drove over a bridge; I couldn't quite read it "*Something* Harbor Crossing." As we came into the city, the sight was spectacular to me. We drove through crowded streets lined with dazzling lights and exquisite buildings. They were tall and all ran together making everything look crowded. It was different from anyplace I had ever seen. It was bright and noisy and stimulating! I saw people walking around freely without fear of someone hurting their family. My thoughts were interrupted as I envisioned Kirima's baby being torn from her arms and Darcy being beaten until she was almost dead; and of me on the cargo ship, eating like an animal. I clinched my fist then spoke the word, "Slave!" I shivered when I thought of what the girls in the barracks had to go through and still were as far as

I knew. Then, Gabriela felt slightly comforted remembering that at least four had escaped into what she prayed was freedom.

The black car pulled up at a tall building that looked like a fancy hotel, except it didn't have a sign in front like many that they had passed on the drive here. The driver stopped, got out and opened Leonidas' door, then mine. Why would a slave be treated with respect? I questioned.

We walked inside and we were greeted by a lovely older woman. "You must be Ella, or would you prefer Gabriela?" She said kindly. "I am Lyn."

"If I get a preference—then, Gabriela." Lyn and I looked at Leonidas. He said, "It really doesn't matter what she calls you now that we're safe in Hong Kong. But *you will be* Ella to Mr. Saku, so remember that! Go ahead and take her to her room, Lyn. We can talk in the morning after we've both had some rest. It's been a long day."

"I can imagine it has Leonidas. Good to have you back." She turned to me and said, "Come with me, Gabriela, I will take you to your new room. It will be home to you for the next few weeks, and then we'll see after that." I followed her, thinking of even more questions that needed an answer. But I knew most would not be answered until my new list was completed.

We entered an elevator and began our assent up to the twelfth floor of the building. Lyn didn't speak until we got off. "This way, Miss Gabriela, your room is just down here, at the end of the hall. She walked slowly, with perfect balance. It looked more like she was floating on air, not walking on ordinary feet. Watching her was intriguing, I thought, *I may end up liking Lyn, even though she is a far cry from my Darcy, she exudes a peaceful presence much like her.*

We stopped in front of a very tall ornate door, and then Lyn placed a key into the lock. It was a gentle but effective reminder that I remained a captive, not an honored guest here. It may be a beautiful door, but it eradicates my freedom the same way the car door did the day of my abduction. I was taken against my will and have remained behind a locked door of sorts ever since. Any semblance of freedom I may have been allowed was just that. I was always guarded and kept on an invisible leash. Truly free...I was not!

We walked through the door and my mouth literally dropped open. I scanned the room in wide-eyed wonder at the vast quarters that I would be staying in. I could never have anticipated this, that's for sure! It was fabulous in every way. I was speechless. Then, all the dazzle of the room was dimmed by the staggering truth; this oversized dramatic room and large comfy bed was just a fancy tent room with a bigger cot! I am here preparing to be nothing more than a sex slave for Saku. I suddenly felt exhausted and longed to be alone.

"Here is your washroom, Gabriela. You should have everything you need to take a nice bath. You will find your robe and slippers behind the door. I think that's all you'll need until I see you in the morning. Oh, yes, there is a phone beside the bed. If you need anything, just pick it up, I will answer momentarily." She saw my look of confusion and patted my hand. "It's a lot to take in, I know. Just enjoy your bath, get some sleep, and we will go over things tomorrow. I'm here to watch over you, so please just try and rest the best you can."

She said good night and left me alone in the massive room. I felt lonely and desired to be back in my familiar tent room. These material comforts were out of my league. I knew nothing of this world. The rundown tent room barracks were more familiar to me, not a place that resembled a palace…. Jose *was* right, I was headed to my next *palace*. However, being here really didn't change anything. I knew who I was, Gabriela Mendoza, and I was by no means a princess, not even close.

All the talk about me being chosen and following my destiny was beyond my comprehension. I was tired and had a headache; my feet were hurting from the new slippers Leonidas gave me to wear and I hate the name Ella! The only thing I wanted to do right now was to enjoy a bath in this ridiculously large tub!

Simple Pleasures

I ran warm water in the deep white tub. Warm water was something I had not felt on my skin in a year. Something like warm water never seemed like a luxurious thing to me until spending an entire year without it. Our shower at home was tiny, but we did have warm water most of the time. I had only experienced a tub bath a few times in my life, even those could hardly equate to the same as this experience.

I undressed and hung my blue dress on a hook behind the bathroom door. I removed my new shoes and dipped my foot into the bath, the water was perfect! I slipped down into the large tub. It felt velvety against my skin, like lying in a large smooth stone. I was suddenly conscious of an unfamiliar calm surrounding me. I savored it, wanting to store it someplace safe, so I could find it again. I closed my eyes to lock it deep in my mind. "Ah, I do hope this is part of Saku's daily list for me!" I immersed my entire body delighting my hair with a long overdue shampooing. The shampoo and soap smelled like coconut—it was intoxicating.

After a long soak, my lack of sleep forced me to leave my new sanctuary. I knew I would retreat to this place often to regain my peace and purity. I didn't know exactly when, but I was certain that both were to be taken from me very soon. I dried off with a towel that was soft and lush. I didn't bother with the robe and slippers. I turned back the sheets of the bed and ran my hand across them. They were soft as grandmother Nuna's orchids. I wrapped my clean body in the petal-like sheets and fell into a restful sleep. I vowed not to think of anything but how wonderful I felt as this very moment.

I woke up with Lyn sweetly coaxing me to eat the breakfast she had brought and sat on the table next to my bed. "You were sleeping very soundly. I've been standing here for a while urging you to open your eyes, Gabriela. You must have needed the rest badly. I know the trip was tiring. You can have a long nap later today, but now, up you go!" She reached to help me sit up while adjusting the pillows behind me.

"I'm having breakfast in bed?"

"Sure, why not? What's the difference between sitting here in your comfy bed, or walking a few feet over to the table to sit?" She pointed to a round table with white linens that hung to the floor. I had missed its presence completely last night.

"You won't hear me complain. The only time I ever got to eat in bed as a child was when I was sick and grandmother Nuna would serve me hot soup."

She placed a tray that fit neatly across my legs. On it were fruit juice, buttered wheat toast, two hard-boiled eggs, and a large bowl of fresh fruit, which, to my delight, included mango.

There was also a small pitcher of hot tea, which I chose *not* to have today! "This is a feast, Lyn. Everything smells delicious." I muttered while biting into the buttered toast.

"There's some sugar to sprinkle over your fruit if you like. I don't think we have to worry about extra calories for you. You may need to put a few pounds before you are ready, but I haven't got a good look at you just yet. Go on enjoy your breakfast in peace. I will lay out your clothes for today." She opened a door and entered another room, but continued talking to me.

"I think we have plenty of choices for you now. But soon, the seamstress will have this closet filled with your very own wardrobe. Aha…this is what I was looking for, and these shoes will do perfect for the day I have planned. When you are finished eating, just freshen up, then put on those things I laid out for you. There's a hairbrush in the drawer on the left side of the vanity. Just pull it back into a ponytail for now. Later, I will give it a thorough brushing. We'll work on some kind of style… much later. Gabriela, eat up, you are going to be busy today!"

I have to be dreaming. I'm as far away from the barracks as one could get! I must have landed on an entirely different planet. Just yesterday, I woke up and made rice and tea in a common brothel for thirty-two prostitutes. What am I doing here in this place? How can my mind possibly transition from the deprivation of that life to the indulgences of this one in just twenty-four hours? It is impossible! I can't do it. I don't know how to do… this chosen girl thing.

What were they thinking of bringing me here, to all of *this*? I can't be what Mr. Saku is expecting. Just what is he expecting anyway? That I'm going to be blown away by all of his wealth and forget everything I have seen this past year? I couldn't, even if I wanted to! The images, the sounds, the smell, the stories of brutality, the degrading treatment of my sisters, will forever remain in my mind. This place and its bewitching beauty will not erase the agony I have witnessed. I am Gabriela Mendoza, no matter what my passport says. I am the Filipino girl who misses her family and her sisters from the barracks.

The Pocket

Darcy was finally well enough to be reassigned. It took longer than she anticipated for her leg to get strong enough to put her full weight on it. "Gettin' old Darcy!" she scolded herself. But her passion in helping to rescue suffering young girls pushed her to keep going. The new assignment would start soon. She pondered the last one thoughtfully. "I met some amazin' girls in Malaysia! I'm sorry I had to leave sa soon!" Darcy despised leaving a job before it was completed. But she knew she was fortunate to get out when she did. Jose was sure to kill her if her identity was compromised as they suspected.

Her mind went back to the night of the escape. She went right past Gabriela's tent room without saying goodbye. She knew it was hard enough on her without dragging it out more. She and Kirima had quietly walked passed Nathan who was drunk from the bottle of tuba Darcy had given him earlier in the day, taken from Jose's stash while he was out bargaining for new girls. He needed to replace twelve, fourteen, and Senegal, as well as several of the others who were getting weaker by the day.

Once they made it out the front door, a van was waiting to pick them up just down the street a ways. Kirima was a big help to Darcy as they hurried to the van praying no one had heard them leave. The pain in her leg was still excruciating. They got in the van and quickly fled as fast and far as they could get from the barracks. The organization wanted to get them completely out of the city as soon as possible. This ring of sex traffickers had men everywhere. It would be almost impossible for them to escape once Jose realized they were gone. Darcy prayed that Leo could talk Jose out of beating Gabriela to tell what she knew.

Darcy could not help but feel proud of Gabriela choosing Kirima to go instead of herself. "Ah, but I do miss the sweet one, though," she reminisced. However, she knew Kirima was the right choice. "She's back in India by now, more than likely rockin' her babe. I wouldn't dare wanna be the man who stole that child from her!" She smiled at the sight of Kirima kicking and fighting for her baby; probably beating the man with a club of some kind. "He certainly had it comin' to him that's fer certain."

But the best news of all was when she heard that the authorities raided the brothel and that all the girls were set free! They had found Pavel's body washed up along the banks of the river. When they searched his body, they discovered a note wrapped in a plastic bag tucked into his pocket. Someone had scribbled the address of the brothel on a page torn from a Bible. Along with the address, they had written, "Please rescue!" That's all that the note said. The police decided to follow up on the lead. After watching the building for a few days, they knew what was going on inside.

Jose and his guards were apprehended along with a few others. Nathan turned on all of them, hoping to make a deal for a lighter sentencing. It was fantastic news to the underground rescue effort, getting one of Saku's ringleaders was huge. They had tried to find ways to get to Saku for years. No one knows where he is, let alone gotten a glimpse of him. His identity has remained a mystery. Men arrested who worked for him admitted never even meeting him. They bragged, "He allows very few to have access, his security is indestructible! There is no way you will ever get to him!"

No one knew who had placed the note in Pavel's pocket; it didn't matter really. Darcy was just thankful that there were twenty-eight girls given their freedom after the raid. And that each of them had a way to provide for themselves besides begging or prostitution, thanks to Gabriela's circle school.

The Reunion

Kirima could not wait a minute longer once things had cooled down. As soon as they could make arrangements for her, she wanted to begin the long journey back to India. The organization provided the money for her to go, but could not offer to escort her. She would have to make the trip alone. Darcy was in good hands and it was time for Kirima to find her baby girl. She was determined to let nothing stop her from rescuing the child and punishing the evil man who tore her from her arms. That moment was deeply etched on her heart and mind, giving Kirima the determination to go on living. She knew this day would come!

The trip to Bihar was long and tedious. Just getting to India from Malaysia was difficult enough. But the journey through India to Bihar got even more complex. Women were not allowed to travel at will, so she had to conceal the fact that she was a female. She rode on numerous trains, taxied through crowded cities being delayed for hours by cows deciding to block the road. The roads outside of town were full of potholes and at times, the car was swept away by flashfloods due to tremendous downpours. But none of these altered her path to Bihar. She kept being pushed forward by a force that could not be seen by human eyes. She moved a little closer to her daughter each day. There were those who Kirima knew must be angels who came to her aid by offering food when she had run out, or an occasional safe place to rest. Then finally, after three months of traveling, she was home.

She decided to continue her disguise and remain a man. She wanted to take her past rapist by surprise. She watched the small shanty of a house from a building nearby. Kirima barely recognized the four children she had cared for playing in front. They had changed a lot. It had been almost four years since she had seen them last. The oldest three were boys, they would be all right no matter what. It was a man's world in India, but the little girl was barely one when Kirima was brought to care for them, what would become of her after tonight? Kirima soon became pregnant and had her baby that first year, which meant her daughter would be about four now.

Kirima knew what she would have to do and was prepared to do it. These four years had given her plenty of time to plan her retribution; all she had to do was get her daughter and get to a safe place.

Fortunately, she knew his routine and doubted he changed it. He was a stupid and evil man, which Kirima counted on to carry out her plan. Every night after he ate, he would come outside and drink until he was drunk. Then, he would go to the side of the house and relieve himself before going back in to force himself on her. It seemed like just yesterday!

She waited until it was dark, then walked quietly toward the house. She peeked into the window and saw a woman, two boys, and two little girls who looked about the same size. Which girl was hers? Would Kirima be able to recognize her? The baby girl that Kirima had taken care of when she was here was named Sonna. She tried to get a better look but didn't want to be seen.

"I can hear them talking, what are they saying?" Then one of boys called out,"Sonna!"

"Oh, please only let Sonna walk to him! Just one of you go—okay? Please?" Kirima spoke softly. He called her name again, "Sonna!"

"Which little girl was going to respond? Oh, God, let me see which girl is mine."

Then one of the girls turned and walked to her brother. He pulled her hair and laughed. Kirima could barely keep from shouting in delight when she saw that the other little girl didn't move; she was still sitting on the floor playing!

"That would be *my baby*, that's my daughter! I thought I might not have a way to recognize her, but now I know for sure, it's her." Kirima strained to see her more clearly. "She is thin and her hair is curly like mine. She is wearing a yellow shirt. I now know for sure which girl to grab when it's time. Okay, I'm ready! Now, Mr. robber-of-virgins come out and get the surprise I have for you."

Kirima waited on the side of the house for him to get good and drunk. "I know he can't last much longer; he will have to get up pretty soon now." Then he got up and began walking to the side of the house, just like he did when she lived there. She remembered lying in bed listening to his every move. Step, step, step, there were eighteen of them, then the sound of him peeing on the ground. She remembers her heart pounding, knowing what was coming next.

"But not tonight; tonight you will get what's coming to you! I've been waiting a long time for this, you, demon," she vowed.

Kirima watched him walk to the same spot beside the house. He reached one hand beneath his long tunic and then braced himself against the house with the other. "*Perfect, just like I planned*," she mused in her head.

Kirima took a firm grip on the iron pipe that she had acquired along her journey here. It had been inconvenient at times to carry in her pack, but now it was going to pay off. She crept up behind him like a lioness about to destroy an unsuspecting prey, then with all the force of her body, she struck him on the back of the head. It stunned him enough for her to get a second blow. This time he fell to the ground. Lying there unprotected, Kirima began beating him with the iron pipe. When she wasn't hitting him with the pipe, she was kicking him in his gut and genitals repeatedly. The loud sound of his bawling and iron pipe whacking against his body brought the woman from inside the house to see what was happening.

At the sight of Kirima beating her husband, she ran toward them, and then began kicking the man lying on the ground with vengeance equal to Kirima's. Both young women continued the attack with vicious hitting and kicking even though the beating had already left him unconscious. When their vengeance was fully satisfied, they stopped and stared at their lifeless offender. The other young woman fell to her knees holding on to Kirima's legs, and began crying and thanking her repeatedly. "Oh, thank you, sweet angel, thank you, thank you for helping us all, thank you!" She was trembling and kissing Kirima's feet. Kirima reached down to help her up, and then their eyes met. Tears of joy began to stream down the faces of both victims, realizing their abuser was a dead man. Both women had been liberated— he was no longer to be feared.

The young woman broke the silence and said, "I am Delia. I know you must be Kirima. He spoke disdainfully of your resistance many times! Each time I heard your name I thought, she is a brave girl and I hope she comes back and kills you one day! I wanted many times to possess your courage, but I feared him too much." They hugged once more then realized they were not alone. They looked toward the house and realized all five of the children had witnessed the murder of their father. The two older boys walked toward the women. Kirima braced herself for another encounter, but instead received a fierce embrace.

"You are Kirima, aren't you? You are our Kirima come back to rescue us, just like you always did when we were little!" Their reaction was something Kirima was not prepared for. Their arms felt tight around her, they had become young men. The taller of the two stood back looking at her and said, "It is you!"

"Yes, it is, I am pleased to know you remember me....I am back! It is good to see that you both are well." Then Kirima stood tall and with a proud and haughty glare said, "I came to get my daughter back."

The oldest boy said pointing, "She's there, the one with the yellow shirt! Go to her, she knows about you. We have told her *often about her brave mother* and that one day she would come to get her." Then the two brothers almost instinctively reached down to pick up their dead father.

"Go quickly into the house, we will take care of the body. He is a worthless piece of dung; he will never get to hurt anyone else...thanks to you, Kirima!" The two women nodded for the boys to take the body, not knowing or caring what the boys intended doing with it. He was dead, that was all they needed to know.

Kirima glanced toward the three children still watching from a distance. She regretted they had to witness the brutal scene. Suddenly, three very grateful children started walking shyly toward her, the one in the yellow shirt lagging behind. The boy reached out and hugged Kirima first then turned and said to the girls. "This is our Kirima, you don't remember her, but she was our mother before Delia."

Kirima hugged the little girl she remembered caring for as a one-year-old infant, now a pretty five year old. Then, Kirima's eye caught the sight of a shy little brown face peering around her big sister. Kirima got down on her knees and said, "It's okay, come here, let me see you. The little girl ran to Kirima, throwing herself into her arms and said one word that Kirima had prayed to hear for the past four years—"Mama!"

The reunion was a sight to behold. Both Kirima and the little girl laughed and cried tears of ecstatic joy while Delia and the other two children laughed with delight. Delia held on to the children with one arm while holding the other up toward the sky repeatedly saying, "I thank you, Lord, for bringing us this day, this is a day of rejoicin'. We thank you! Thank you!"

Finally, Delia said, "We better go inside, even though no one around here pays any attention to screams coming from this house. It's what they expect to hear." It was clear the man had continued beating his wife and helpless children. It was hard to fathom that no one was willing to defend this family from his abuse all these years.

Once inside, Kirima realized she had blood splattered all over her. Holding up her bloodied bruised hands, she asked, "Is there a place I can…ah, clean up?" Delia smiled reassuringly and said, "It's atonement blood Kirima, nothing to be ashamed of. I'll get you some water and towels. I believe I can find something for you to wear. Wait here."

Kirima looked at her little girl then realized she didn't even know her name. "What's your name? What should I call you?" The little girl's eyes fell to the floor, and her sister answered for her. "He had us call her, "Nothing."

"You mean you couldn't say her name or call to her or… speak to her? Kirima asked, needing clarification.

"No, her name is *Nothing*. He told us when she was a baby to call her *Nothing*, because she was nothing, just like her mother. We were badly beaten if we ever called her anything but that name. We could not even call her, Sister!"

Kirima's heart broke into a million pieces when she realized the humiliation her child must have endured these past four years.

"He wouldn't let her eat with us, either; she only got the scrapes that were left over," Delia admitted as she brought the water to Kirima.

"But we all saved stuff for her," the young girl confessed innocently.

"It's true; we *all* hid food in our clothes and gave it to her later, when he wasn't looking," the brother declared in defense.

"Well, I'd say you were all very brave, and that you, little one, the bravest of all. Come to me." Kirima looked lovingly into the eyes of her little girl, remembering the unforgettable moment she was pulled from her arms. "I am pleased that he waited for *me*, your mother, to name you. I am going to give you the most beautiful name I have ever heard. Your name is…Gabriela."

"Gabriela?" the girl said reverently. She smiled with the dignity of a queen who had just received a long awaited crown.

"Yes, my Gabriela. And I am also going to call you *my treasure* for this day." She said in honor of her friend who had just proven to Kirima *there was always a way to find a treasure in each day if you would only search for one.* Kirima's search ended today, finding her treasure for this day and all her days to come.

New List

Gabriela finished what she could on her tray and instructed Lyn not to take it just yet. She tried to eat more, but the scanty diet of rice and tea limited Gabriela's stomach from eating all she wanted.

"Gabriela, you can eat anytime you choose. All you have to do is ask," Lyn said confidently.

"But hurry if you are going to eat more. I need you to get dressed soon. I have important information to tell you."

"I'll dress; I am completely full for now. Is that what you want me to put on?" she asked, pointing at the outfit lying on the bed beside her. It was a lightweight cotton shirt with slouchy pants. Her new sneakers remained neatly on the floor, just waiting for Gabriela to take possession of them.

"Yes, comfort before beauty today. Take advantage of it, it will be short lived," Lyn warned.

Gabriela pulled back the sheets, revealing her naked body. Lyn glanced her way and Gabriela felt a sudden shyness come over her as this stranger stared at her nude body. Lyn recognized the embarrassment of her new trainee.

"Gabriela, dear, you're going to have to get use to your bare body being exposed to me, I will know everything about you, even things you have not yet discovered about yourself!" Lyn smiled to herself knowing this honest modesty would work in her favor one day soon. *One less thing on the list that I must teach her before her time with Saku*, she thought with satisfaction.

Gabriela slipped out of bed and quickly put on the clothes Lyn had chosen for her. She sat on the bed then tied her shoes. "Everything fits perfectly!" she said perplexed.

"Leonidas rarely gets anything wrong, including surmising the exact size of a beautiful girl!" Lyn bragged.

"Oh, so he's obviously done this a few times."

"He certainly has, although I don't remember him actually escorting one here himself. You're the first."

Gabriela wasn't sure how Lyn expected her to take that comment; she definitely wouldn't call her trip here with Leonidas…being escorted. "More like forced and taken against her will. Escorting didn't usually involve threats against your life, did they?" she argued to herself.

"Okay, Lyn, I'm dressed. Can I take a moment in the washroom?"

"Sure…I don't mean to rush you, dear, it's just you are a few weeks behind the others in your preparation. Leonidas wants me to hurry you along. So, go on. I'm sorry to sound so bossy. I'm usually not. I'll wait here. I want you to pull your hair back again. You won't be seeing anyone but me today.

Gabriela closed the door behind her then looked at herself in the ornate mirror bearing her image. "I have not seen my full reflection since I left home for work…that day. I remember closing the washroom door to look into the mirror Papa had placed on the back of it. He bought it for mother's birthday one year. I look so skinny in these clothes." She gently ran her hands across her thin torso. Then she stopped abruptly at her breasts, noticing they had changed during the past year. She stared into the eyes of the girl looking back at her, "What is going to happen to you, Gabriela? Who are these strange people? How and why did they choose you? What is the purpose behind all of this? You are a young girl from a poor family in the Philippines. You are no great beauty, or have anything unusual to offer this man! But I swear to you, I will help you keep your dignity through this, and you will remain strong and not allow them to destroy who you truly are—no matter what it costs—I swear to you today, do you hear me, Gabriela? I swear!" After she finished making these promises to herself, she splashed water on her face. She washed her hands with the coconut-scented soap, and then walked out to hear what Lyn had to say about Mr. Saku's new list.

"I'm ready, Lyn."

"Come here and sit at the table with me, dear. I will tell you what is going to be happening to you for the next few weeks, and then I will be happy to answer your questions, is that fair?"

Gabriela wanted to scream, "Fair? Nothing has been fair since the day I was pushed into a stranger's car and forced onto a cargo ship then locked in the tent room barracks! No, Lyn, no matter how sweet you try and make this sound, this is not fair." But screaming at her would change nothing for her presently, so instead, she walked to the table and said, "That sounds fine."

Gabriela sat down at the linen-clad table across from the attractive older woman. She looked into her eyes hoping to see what was behind them. "Who was she? If she is as kind and caring as she appears, why would she work for such a man as Saku doing this sort of work for him?" she silently questioned.

Lyn paused…waiting for her young trainee to get comfortable and then began. "Gabriela, you are here for one sole purpose: to be prepared to become one of seven girls who are to serve Mr. Saku in any way he chooses. This is not his first harem of girls; he has had many through the years. After he has become bored with his present harem, he demands that new girls be found. He always chooses seven, although nothing else remains consistent. Some girls stay with him for several years while others last only a few months. He is a man with great…appetites which are not easily satisfied."

Gabriela frowned at the thought of being trained in some type of sexual expertise so that she would please him; however, Lyn quickly put an end to those thoughts as she continued.

"I am not here to train you to be an expert in satisfying him with your great sexual competence. His attraction to women has many facets. So, I will train you to be captivating, beguiling, and alluring to always keep him fascinated with you. There are many, many beauties in the world, but very few are truly *beautiful,"* she spoke, saying the word almost melodic.

"For the past eleven months, your soul and spirit were being trained. The list was given to teach you humility, compassion, self-denial, worldliness, and injustice. You always had these hidden in your heart, Gabriela, but the list was to reveal whether or not you would give them permission to take over and rule your life. This is what Leonidas was there to witness: to observe if you would allow these virtues to surface and control you. If so, then you would be chosen to continue."

Lyn reached across the table and patted Gabriela's hand, "I know your time there was very hard, but Leonidas told me how exceptional you were. He called here often to tell of your progress and each time he was more impressed than the last. You have made quite an impression on Leonidas, and that, my dear, is difficult to accomplish."

"Now, let me get back to your training here. You know you are in Hong Kong. This building is Mr. Saku's personal residence. He lives in the pent house on the top floor. No one is ever permitted to go there. He will visit you in a suite assigned to you...you will see it soon enough. I am to teach you proper etiquette so when you join him for dinner or evenings out to his clubs you will behave like a very sophisticated woman, not a child."

"You will be served a strict diet to keep you lean and firm, although I think perhaps the stairs down to the kitchen and up again several times a day might have taken care of that. I will decide about that later after I have a thorough look at you." She stopped briefly, taking a moment to glance at Gabriela. "You will have special beauty treatments for your entire body, Gabriela. You will have skin like a delicate petal; soft and lightly scented. A seamstress will design a wardrobe just for you. You are going to be more beautiful than you could have ever imagined."

Lyn finally stopped and studied her. "This is a lot for you to think about. There is more, but that is for Leonidas to discuss with you later. I will answer your questions, go ahead, I'm listening."

"I can only think of one just now, Lyn. What happens if I don't please him?"

"You do not have to worry about that, Gabriela. I have trained many girls for Mr. Saku through the years, and I can assure you, everything about you will be pleasing to him. Now, if that's all, let's get started. And, Gabriela, feel free to ask me anything if you should think of something later. I will tell you what I can."

That day, Lyn would begin teaching her new trainee the art of walking on air. It was much more of a skill than Gabriela imagined. The following weeks were filled with mineral salt baths, full body massages to rub exotic oils deep into her flawless brown skin. There were numerous fittings with the seamstress who often took Gabriela's ideas when choosing patterns and fabric. She learned how to hold on to Saku's arm when entering a room with him; how to sit next to him or across from him, eating with impeccable manners. She mastered getting into a limousine and exiting like a lady; how to drink fine wine and sip expensive champagne, how to tolerate caviar and other despicable foods. Then, one morning, Lyn woke her and said, "Gabriela, I think you are ready...to hear from Leonidas."

The Truth

Leonidas watched Gabriela almost daily from afar. He knew his hunch was right the day he saw her working at Miss Lolani's shop. She would be a perfect choice; Saku would not be able to resist her captivating beauty. Even without makeup and unsophisticated style, she was breathtaking. In fact, if it was his choice—and it wasn't—he wouldn't change anything about her. He even thought her cocky arrogance was appealing. He laughed out loud thinking of her lugging rice and tea up the horrendous stairs every day. And the sight of that ridiculous sling flung across her back to help carry the rice easier, was especially endearing to him.

He was impressed with her idea of the circle school and wanted to do more, but could not risk someone noticing him starting to care for her. This was most definitely not part of the plan. Get her through the first part of the list, and if she passed, then bring her here. No one had ever gotten this far before. Sure, there were others they had hopes for, but all of them failed in one way or another. None of them met all the requirements to be *the chosen one*. Until now, Gabriela had achieved the lofty goal. She was *the one* and his feelings for her did not matter. She has accomplished everything on the list. He knew it was time for her to hear everything.

Leonidas spoke with Lyn and asked her to arrange the meeting for later that evening in Gabriela's room. He was prepared to tell her everything, except how he felt about her, of course. There was no room for sentiment with so much at stake. He had waited many years for the opportunity to present the plan to *the chosen one*.

Lyn knocked at Gabriela's door before coming in. "Gabriela, I know it's been a long day, but Leonidas wants to come and speak with you later. I wanted to warn you in case you decided to bathe and turn in early."

"Leonidas, huh? So, am I to hear about the rest of the list tonight…the part you said that he would have to tell me?"

"Yes, he is coming to talk with you about the list. So, that will be all right with you? You'll be expecting him, right?" Gabriela thought it strange that Lyn was asking for her permission. That was what she was doing, wasn't it? Or was she there for another reason?

147

"Sure, I've been wondering when he would talk with me about it. I've known it was coming, I might as well hear what's next for me."

"Do you want me to lay something out for you to change into? You've been in that dress all day."

"Well, if you think I need to, but he's certainly seen me look worse!" she laughed.

"Oh, well then, if you're fine with that dress, I just thought you might want to freshen up for your meeting, but never mind, if you are comfortable then I'll just leave. You have about an hour before he will arrive. Good night, I'll see you tomorrow."

After Lyn closed the door, Gabriela walked to the mirror and took assessment of her dress. If Lyn thought I should change, I'm sure it was for a reason; she always has a reason. She went to her wardrobe closet and viewed her choices. Choices…she hadn't had any of those lately. "I like this pink one; it's simple and nice enough." She quickly changed then brushed her hair, noticing it was very shiny and had gotten longer. "All these beauty treatments paid off, I suppose," she admitted to herself. Walking to her favorite overstuffed chair, Gabriela picked up a magazine then sat down looking through it absentmindedly. Her thoughts were running wild wondering what Leonidas was coming to tell her. Then she heard his knock at the door.

The knock startled her, causing her to jump to her feet. She was glad he hadn't seen her reaction; she never liked giving Leonidas the upper hand. Gabriela, wanting to appear calm, walked slowly to the door. She took a deep breath and opened the door.

"Sorry for coming so late in the day, but I needed to take care of some stuff for the boss." Gabriela rolled her eyes. "Yes, I have a boss, too, don't forget that!" Leonidas said defensively.

"Yes, I am very well aware of your boss, Mr. Saku. You probably need to come in, right? I'm guessing this meeting is not going to be a brief one."

"Yes, I do need to come in, and no, it will not be brief." He said with a lengthy sigh.

"Come in and sit down? You want the table or prefer my comfy chairs?"

"Table is fine."

They sat down, both being noticeably anxious. Gabriela was anxious about what she was about to hear and Leonidas, angry at himself for having fallen for her. He reminded himself he was there to give her the rest of the list. He cleared his throat and began.

"Well, Gabriela, let me say: First of all, what you are about to hear, no other girl has heard. There has never been a girl who has successfully completed the *entire list* allowing her to arrive at this particular place."

What was he talking about? Lyn said there had been many girls chosen for numerous harems through the years. Leonidas sat back in his chair and continued.

"So, I am going to make you an offer. After hearing this part of the list, if you do not wish to continue on, you will be freed from becoming part of Saku's harem."

Gabriela sat up in her chair and gasped. "What did you say? I can just leave here if I don't like this last part of the list?"

"No, I did not say you could just leave here, I said you would not have to be in his harem. If you choose not to continue, you

will be taken care of in a place far away from here, under...
protection living as Ella Muñoz."

"I'm listening, Leonidas, just tell me!"

"Okay, but I have a lot to say and I'm going to ask you NOT
to interrupt until I am completely finished. I know how hard that
is for you to do, but please just listen to me."

"I promise not to interrupt, just talk, you're making me
crazy!"

"You have some idea of who this man Mr. Saku is, but you
do not really know who I am. So, let me explain about myself
first." Leonidas pushed his chair back from the table and stood
up, paced for a moment then sat back down. "All of this is pretty
bizarre, but I have to start somewhere, so here goes! I have been
forced to work for Saku for over seventeen years. I met him when
I was just eighteen. He made me the same deal I made you on the
flight here. If I didn't do exactly as he ordered, my family would
be brutally murdered. I have despised every assignment he has
ever given me. I am ridden with guilt every waking hour for
approving the abduction of many innocent girls on his behalf.

I met a man about ten years ago that I became close friends
with. He also worked for Saku under the exact circumstances
that I did. We spent hours late at night for months trying to find
a way to destroy him. Perhaps that sounds easy to you, I mean I
see him all the time, why not just poison the guy, right? Not the
solution! There are a hundred others waiting to take over who
are just as evil. It would only slow things down for a while by
just stopping him.

We had to a find a way to get the others as well, at least
the ones who are in *the group*. His words, not mine. He is
constantly leaving for secret meetings with the group. We have

not managed to find where they meet or who is in this group. He has connections all over the world. If he leaves with one driver, he changes to another several times, before reaching one of his private jets. That he flies to destination X! Gabriela, the best agents from every country around the world have tried to crack this group—no one has been successful. We knew we needed his list of names, his contacts, and bank account numbers. We had to have everything to wipe out as many of them as we could. We risked our lives by sneaking into his pent house when he is out of town numerous times, hoping to find information. We dug through his trash pouring over meaningless scraps of paper, searched through books, tore the room apart, but found no clues whatsoever. All of this done without being caught; he is meticulous about his things. We were putting ourselves, as well as our families in danger, only to come up with nothing."

Gabriela could not stand to hold her tongue another minute. "Leonidas, I'm sorry, I said I wouldn't interrupt but I have to say something! This must be some crazy story you are making up to scare me into being afraid of him, or a test of my intelligence to see if I'm gullible! Tell me this isn't real—or is it?"

"It is real, Gabriela. Our Mr. Saku is one of the most powerful criminals in the entire world. You already know about his activity in prostitution. Prostitution is one thing, but he specializes in buying and selling human beings. It's called human trafficking. But his criminal involvement goes way beyond these; he runs many destructives vices. He is the *Criminal Lord* himself, everything illegal in Eurasia must go through him. From smuggling illegal arms, funding nuclear weapons, counterfeiting, and drug rings around the world, he's got his hands in all of it one way or another."

Leonidas got up from the table and began pacing around the room.

"He got his start by smuggling diamonds. That's when he and Pavel met. Pavel was part of a small time operation in Russia when he told Saku about the money to be made there. Saku's lust for more sucked him in. But once he became part of that world, the truth of who he really was came out. Saku was born into wealth. He was the only son of a successful business man in Japan."

"But why would anyone who has so much need more?" she questioned. "I can't understand what one person needs with all this money anyway."

"It stopped being about the money a long time ago, Gabriela. Now, it's the power that intoxicates him."

"Lyn warned me about that. Okay, I believe what you are saying is true. This guy, Saku, is scum, he needs to be stopped, but why are you telling me? What is it, Leonidas, that I was chosen for, I mean *really* chosen for?"

"We need someone to get close enough to him to find his list."

Gabriela interrupted again. "Ah, *his list*, huh? So, *Mr. Saku's list* has nothing to do with all the stuff you have been having me do this past year, does it? You want me to help you get his list?"

"Well, yes and no. Saku started handing me a list years ago describing in detail what women he wanted me to bring him. Everyone in his organization knew I was working for him; my job was to find women on Mr. Saku's list. That's what gave us, and I say us, because now there is actually an army of people in our movement trying to take him down. Like I was saying, that gave us the idea to find the perfect girl, one who could captivate him so completely that maybe he would let down his guard. Perhaps tell her, or maybe she could discover where he hid his list containing everything we need to take down, not just one man, but hundreds of them."

"And you think I am this perfect girl…because?"

"Gabriela, we knew the girl needed to be more than beautiful. She needed to show she was smart, had guts. She had to prove she was willing to trade her life, her freedom for others to go free. To work hard. To be willing to do what she was told, even if she hated it. She needed to prove she could keep secrets, and tell very convincing lies when they were needed. She needed to experience pain and suffering. She needed to witness these injustices with her own eyes."

The Choice

"That's why you took me to the brothel; to see what the girls had to do, but not have to do them myself? The list was to show you if I would do the work?"

"Work was part of it, and you did work hard! But you proved a lot more to me, Gabriela. You wanted to help these girls do more than just go free, you wanted them to *be free*. The circle school was genius. Then, when you could have left and ran from all of that with Darcy, you didn't. You chose someone else. That's when I knew for sure you were definitely *the chosen one* to do this job.

"But, you don't have to. You can choose not to do this, Gabriela."

"It's not a matter of me not choosing to do it, Leonidas. I have no idea why you think I can! Just because I made rice and tea for some helpless prostitutes doesn't qualify me for this!"

"You gave them much ***more than rice***, Gabriela, all of them. You gave them hope."

"I want to help, Leonidas—I do—but what if I fail you, you and the others?"

"You won't! Because when you are afraid and want to quit, you will remember the faces of the girls in the barracks. You will remember *their* stories! That's why you started the circle in the first place; so they would have a voice. Those faces represent over more than twelve million people who are held in bondage of forced labor. They are slaves in one form or another! Gabriela, I am certain you will not quit! I saw you get enraged over the death of one young girl who bled to death because of a botched up abortion. There are reports that prove over one million children in Asia alone are held against their will, being forced to do whatever their owners demand they do, with millions more being taken every year.

"When you feel like you cannot stomach Saku touching you one more time, you will close your eyes and remember his drug lords that prey on the innocent, getting them addicted to drugs then force them to sell those same drugs to even younger victims."

He stopped and looked intently at Gabriela.

"There's a lot to consider, Leonidas," Gabriela sighed.

"Yes, I realize you need time for all of this to sink in. I apologize that I had to lay it all on you at once. But we couldn't risk you knowing of our plans until we were certain you could be trusted. I am truly sorry for not being able to tell you the truth.

But, *the teacher doesn't speak during the examination.* I had to know if you could pass the test.

"You are right; I need some time alone to consider your offer. I will think about it and let you know tomorrow. And Leonidas, I am sorry about your family. I do hope they are safe."

"Thank you, they are for now."

Leonidas left and Gabriela walked to her bed and fell to her knees.

For a long while, she cried tears of compassion about what she had just heard. Then her crying turned into sobbing—begging for the answer she needed—asking God why she had been chosen. Her wailing was interrupted when she thought she heard a voice. Startled, she turned to see who had entered her room without her knowing.

"Who is it? Who is there?" She saw a small child, a girl standing just a few feet from her. "Who are you, how did you get in here?"

"Gabriela, don't be afraid, it's me, Dalisay, your sister."

Gabriela turned back to the bed and hid her face in the fragile fabric covering of her bed. "Okay, Gabriela, you're just under a lot of stress, collect yourself, there is no one there."

"Yes, there is, I just told you, I am here, now turn around so you can see for yourself. I know you've seen many pictures of me, look…it's me!" The child held out her arms then twirled around to face Gabriela with a wide-eyed smile.

"Dalisay, I don't understand. What are you? Are you an angel of some sort? Are you my imagination, or what?"

"I am not an angel, I am me! I have been asked to watch over you lately."

"Been asked to…by who?"

155

"Well, by everyone in the family for starters, not that people on earth decide what we do while we are in heaven. But this time, their prayers were answered and I was sent by a higher authority, God Himself. He said you needed a lot of help from me. So, that's what I've been doin'!" she said playfully.

"Helping...how?"

"Lots of ways really, but mostly making sure you were safe. I tried to let you know a few times that I was watching out for you, but you didn't seem to notice."

"Like when?"

"Like bringing you your favorite fruit, mango, and coconut milk for the rice. I'm the voice you heard in your tiny kitchen that day asking, "What are *you* going to do about it?" I thought for sure you would figure that one out. Then there was the blue dress with puff sleeves that I whispered to Leonidas when he was picking out a dress for you, and by the way, I had nothing to do with the shoes," she giggled.

"Dalisay, you died, how you can be so happy and even silly? I mean...you're dead...aren't you? You are some sort of spirit floating around, sad to leave your family and stuff like that, or at least that's how I've always thought of you."

"Nope! Not sad, definitely not sad. And Gabriela, people don't really...die. They live on, though in another place. And I am in a spectacular place, just having fun waiting for all my family who will join me one day. Oh, yeah, and I'm actually not alone here now; Grandmother Nuna is here as well. She came here right after you left on your journey. We had the best time when she first arrived! It was way cool."

"So, how come I can see you now, but I haven't before, the other times you were with me?"

"Well, we don't get to appear very often, sad to say, just on very special occasions, when nothing else will do. This is one of those times, little sister. You will always be my little sister, even though you are older, that's crazy, huh?"

"So, big sister, you have some answers for me? I am scared and don't know if I can do what they expect of me. I want to help, but can I?"

"You can do anything for love Gabriela, you have already proven you love others who are weak and need help. This has always been your destiny."

"What? To be here with Mr. Saku? This is my destiny?"

"Your destiny was to give your life for others, because it was first done for you."

"What do you mean, Dalisay? I can't follow what you are trying to tell me."

"You wouldn't remember—you were only about a year old when it happened."

"What happened?"

"It was a cool day; I remember that part really well. Cool days in Manila, well you know those are rare. I was in the house wiping the windows when I saw mother take you outside. She took you to Miguel; he was playing with his marbles under our big mimosa tree. He was good at marbles, he used to come home from school with new ones every day. He got in trouble all the time from Papa for playing keepsies. Anyway, you were at that age, about one, where you loved running and having people chase you. You were so happy all the time, Gabriela, I hope you are happy again soon."

"So what happened, Dalisay? What happened that day?"

157

"You took off running like always, but Miguel wasn't paying attention. I saw you, though; you were running toward the street in front of the house. I screamed for Miguel to get you, but he just ignored me, so I ran out the door as fast as I could, calling your name telling you to stop, but you thought we were playing and kept running. I saw a car coming and tried to get you out of the way, the car swerved to miss you, but it hit me."

"Oh, Dalisay, you died saving me? I am so ashamed, no one ever told me." Gabriela sobbed hysterically. "I am alive because you died saving me? I understand why mother couldn't love me! How could anyone? Dalisay—sister—please forgive me. You should have lived, not me."

"That is not true, Gabriela; you were saved for a purpose. You have a choice to make as I did, as everyone has—to give to others in ways only you can. That day, you needed someone to risk a life for you. Today, you have the opportunity to do the same thing. Risking your life could quite possibly save thousands... millions, but that doesn't mean my sacrifice was any less. I saved you and because I did, I am now part of something even greater than my life or yours."

"Can you come closer, so I can kiss you?"

"No, you are only allowed to see me, and you may never have another vision of me. But I promise I will be around. It's time for me to leave you, my little sister."

"Please don't go! Are you leaving without telling what to do?"

"You know what to do Gabriela, you have always known what to do, and you'll be fine. I will be there to help you if you can't do it yourself. We are not allowed to do things for people that they can do on their own. But I promise, you will know when I am nearby."

"How will I know, Dalisay, if I can't see you?"

"You will feel peaceful, like when Darcy was speaking to you, or the peace you felt when you first met Lyn. There may be a gust of wind swirl around you or a faint breeze brush your face. It will probably be me, holding you or blowing you a kiss. I have to go, I've already stayed longer than I was instructed to. I love you, little sister, and mother loves you too. She just can't find the way to get it out of her heart to yours."

Before Gabriela could say anything else, she was gone.

The Answer

Gabriela was instantly at peace. Her sister's presence once again calmed her anxiety that only moments ago filled her completely. "I know what I need to do; I know what I want to do." Exhausted, she climbed into bed with the pink dress still on that she had worn for her meeting with Leonidas. She knew tomorrow her life would change dramatically, but now, she needed to sleep.

She woke up early feeling more rested than she had in months. Now that it was settled in her heart, she was full of energy; a new passion fueled her desires. Nothing else mattered right now, just meet Saku and find that list!

Lyn came in with a tray while Gabriela was in the shower. "Gabriela, you are up early, here's your breakfast."

"Thanks!" she answered back. "Could you wait for me to get out? I need to give you something for Leonidas."

"Sure, I'll be right here, don't hurry." In just a few minutes, Gabriela came out in her robe with her hair wrapped up in a towel. "Your beauty amazes me, even like this," she said pointing her hands toward the freshly showered girl.

"You are biased, I think, or proud of your protégée, I'm sure it must be one or the other." She walked to her nightstand and picked up an envelope. "I need you to get this to Leonidas as soon as you can, Lyn. It is very important, and personal. Can you get it to him?"

"Certainly, I'll give it to him right away. He usually has a morning swim, but he should be done by now. I'll check his suite. Do I need to wait for an answer from him? Or should I just leave it with him and go?"

"You don't have to wait, it's something he asked me to do last night at our meeting, and I told him I would let him know today, that's all." She stated matter-of-factly.

Lyn took the note and walked from Gabriela's room to Leonidas's private quarters. She knocked at the door waiting for him to answer. Finally, she heard someone struggling to open the door. "Leonidas, is that you? Are you okay?" When the door opened, Lyn saw Leonidas. He was dressed, but his clothes were rumpled and his hair a mess. It was evident that he had fallen asleep in his clothes. "You okay?"

"Yes, Lyn, come in. I tossed and turned all night."

"Did your meeting with Gabriela not go well?"

"I said what I needed to say, she has a lot to consider today. I doubt she slept a wink herself."

"I just saw her, she looked spectacular! Better than ever—and she gave me this envelope for you."

Lyn held out the envelope, waiting for him to take it. "Leonidas, here, take it!"

"I don't know if I want to read it."

"Why, don't you want to know?"

"All right, but stay, I may need you to make arrangements for her if...well, just stay."

Leonidas held the envelope delicately in his hands. He carefully opened it and removed the card inside. It had one word on it. "Yes!" He sat down and began to cry.

"Leonidas, what? What is the matter, did she decline? What could upset you so much?"

"No, she agreed. I guess realizing what this could mean for so many people just got to me. I mean, I've waited such a long time, and now we have her, the one, you know the chosen *one*."

"Then you should be rejoicing! This should be one of the happiest days of your life."

"It is. I'm sorry Lyn, I think I should get around and shower. I have a lot of things to do today to get things set up." Leonidas walked to his desk to pick up a pad and began writing furiously. "I must make sure the suite is perfect for her first night! I've had years to get ready for this and now I am running out of time. This is really going to happen, Lyn, and I know, she is going to succeed, I just feel it!"

"I believe she will." Lyn said assuring. Then the tone of her voice changed, it sounded almost scolding. "So that's it? You are willing to send her off to a heartless man never knowing that she was ever truly loved? Will you not at least give her that... my son?"

"Mother, I, why did you say that...love her? I don't...can't... will not allow it!"

"Oh, so you think you can control that, too? You have always taken care of everybody else's heartbreak but your own. No mother could ask for a more devoted son. You have done a wonderful job at comforting my heart from the day Saku took my daughters. You stayed here doing what he asked only to protect your sisters. But, Leonidas, you have never taken time for your own heart."

She walked over to him giving him a tender hug and said, "I beg you, do not make this mistake. There is no going back after she is with him. You know the harem is not allowed to leave their suites and no one is to enter except for female servants. There are no exceptions, not even for you." She turned and left him alone to make his decision.

Leonidas stood in the shower bawling like a baby. The water mingled with his tears while streaming down his face. It helped him deny their sting. He was furious with himself." How could I let this happen? I knew from the beginning she was always for him! You are such a fool, Leonidas. You must get her out of your mind!" Then something happened that interrupted his self-lecture. He thought he heard a voice. He stopped and turned off the shower. "Hello, anyone there?"

He looked around and saw no one, but heard a voice quietly within saying, "You didn't let it happen, it was meant to happen and you will only be a fool if you don't tell her how you feel!"

Leonidas, thinking himself to have completely lost his mind, hurried and got dressed to go about his day. "So, now, I'm hearing voices? The stress of this is worse than I thought."

But the voice kept taunting him throughout the day. He could not get the words out of his head. "You're only a fool if you don't tell her."

"All right, I will. I'm going right now. I know she is going to think I've gone insane, but I'll just go right to her and say, 'Hey Gabriela, I know I asked you to risk your life and be with

a scumbag and all, but I just wanted to tell you that I love you!'
That's good, that's tender and convincing! What is she going to
think? Well, I suppose it won't matter much what she thinks, I
won't be seeing her after today anyway."

He stood at her door searching for a better way to say it. But
since he didn't have any previous experience with the words,
I love you, he was at a loss. Waiting there wasn't helping—he
placed his hand on the door and knocked softly.

Gabriela opened the door, "Hello, Leonidas, I was hoping
you would come by after you got my answer. Come in. I want
to talk with you about it." He strolled in on legs that felt like
spaghetti. She was more beautiful today than he had ever seen
her look before. He was smitten, consumed, and helpless to
control his heart. There was no way he could contain his feelings
any longer. He longed for her to know. Just her knowing would
be comforting enough. He had no expectation that she would
feel anything for him.

"Leonidas, I wanted you to know that I'm…"

"Just stop, okay, you can't talk, not this time, no interruptions!
I'm serious, Gabriela!" He warned as she placed her finger to her
lips to mock him.

"Shh, I won't say a word," she teased.

"I need to tell you something that I have kept from you a long
time. I know I can't ever just say things quickly; I've always got
to go back and explain things. But this story you deserve to hear
from the beginning. Sit down and listen to me," he paused and
then began. "I saw you a few weeks before you were taken that
day; you were working at the dress shop. I had heard there was a
wonderful custom dress shop in Manila and since I was there, I
thought I might buy something for my mother…Lyn."

"I knew it! You look just like her! She's always so informal with you, not like the others who work for you…yep, I knew it! That's wonderful, so Lyn is your mother? That's what you came to tell me?"

He shook his head at her for interrupting him, then continued. "I saw you and thought you were the most beautiful thing I had ever laid my eyes on, and I wasn't looking for Saku that day. I noticed you for me." He watched her reaction carefully, and then went on with his story.

"I had other errands to run, but I left thinking I would come back and introduce myself later. As I stepped out of the store, I saw Pavel. I was shocked at seeing him out in broad daylight; since he usually crawled out at night. He saw me and stopped to chat. I had to ask what he was up to before I left him. He told me how he had seen an amazingly beautiful girl, you, the day before while walking and he followed you. He was certain you would bring a very high price in the upcoming *sheik auction* and was staking out the area for your abduction. Terrified for your life, I lied. I told him that he was too late, that you had already been chosen for Mr. Saku. But he could be in charge of making the deal if he wanted—but remember, she is for Saku. He was taking you Gabriela—there was no way to save you. The only way was to keep you with me. I should have known then this day would come."

"What day, Leonidas, we've had a lot of days here lately. What day?"

"The day that I would have to admit that I have been completely consumed with love for you since the moment I laid eyes on you."

Gabriela was silent for a few moments and then said, "Okay, now it's your turn to listen to me. You owe me, Leonidas! I have listened to lengthy lectures and crazy stories about this lunatic Saku that you work for. You have told me what to do, where to go, how to act, what to wear and now I'm telling you. You owe me! You owe me at least a kiss—my first and last real kiss!"

Leonidas walked to her slowly, wanting to take in each detail of this perfect moment. He took her hands and kissed them softly. The same beautiful hands that worked tirelessly for girls in the brothel. He touched her face, something he had desired to do numerous times when they were together in Malaysia. He looked deeply into her eyes knowing that he may never get to look at them like this again. He ran his fingers over her lips. He put his arms around her tiny frame, pressing into him as close as he could, then lifted her face toward him and kissed her with a passion more consummating than either one would ever feel again.

They held each other for a moment, knowing they could not risk another. The kiss was their blessing and was their curse, because they knew to be together would disqualify her from being the chosen one. Some things must die in order to give life to others. Then he spoke the words, "I love you, I will forever. Always know I'm thinking of you. Every night for the rest of my life I will look at the moon and say, I love you, Gabriela."

"And I will answer, I love you, Leonidas." And they said goodbye.

The Liaison

Gabriela looked at herself in the large mirror hanging in the wall of her room. She would be leaving here today, moving into her new suite called *Ella's Place*. She stood contemplating the full meaning of the suite's title. Was it her place, as in her house? Or was it more like *remember your place?* Either way, it is where she would meet Mr. Saku for the very first time and become his.

She wasn't even afraid—Dalisay told her she wouldn't be. It was a wonderful treasure for me to meet her. As Gabriela began pondering the word *treasure,* it reminded her that she had ceased looking for them. "I will start looking again. If I don't look, then I certainly will not find any treasures in my life ever again. I cannot live without treasures!" Some people called them blessings. But "treasure" was the word Gabriela preferred; it made them tangible, something she could hold on to. The word "blessing" reminded her of priests sprinkling water over people that disappeared moments later. All the treasures she collected while at the brothel had a real place in her heart, and they would never disappear.

She heard Lyn knock at the door. "Gabriela, it's time to go. We have a lot to do to get your suite ready for Mr. Saku tonight. I have some thoughts that might interest you in your preparations. You want to hear?"

"Well, of course, Lyn, you know him. I don't have a single idea about what to wear or say or do. Even though I may not have to say or do anything!" she laughed mischievously.

"Let's go. We can talk when we are safe inside. You have absolute privacy when you are in Ella's Place. No one can come in or go out unless you unlock the door, not even me. Remember, I told you there would be a guard posted outside your entrance twenty-four hours a day. He is here already," she pointed out as we stopped in front of Ella's Place.

To step inside the door of Ella's Place was like walking into the home of a wealthy heiress, not a poor Filipino girl. Gabriela walked from room to room with Lyn as her personal guide, showing her how to work the high-tech remote controls of basically everything. The art was exquisite, "All originals," Lyn explained. There were sculptures and paintings, too many to count. There was one that immediately struck at Gabriela's heart. "Lyn, tell me about this painting, it is wonderful! The artist's name is Gustav Klimt, that's right isn't it?" she asked, peering close to read the signature.

"I am not surprised that you noticed that one. It was purchased just two days ago and hung this afternoon. It is called "The Kiss," one of Klimt's most famous. He was obsessed with his young wife who, unfortunately, did not live long. You will see her in a lot of his work."

"Purchased only two days ago?"

"Yes, that's what I was told," she said with a wink.

"Gabriela, it is a beautiful suite. I can continue to see you as much as you would like. You really do not need training anymore. But I am here to make sure you have everything you need or run personal errands, really, whatever you need." As they continued the tour, she abruptly changed the subject.

"Oh, I do have one fun bit of gossip to tell you about a guard who fell in love with one of Saku's girls. They met secretly in the middle of the night many times a week. I doubt anyone would have ever found out about it, except she became pregnant. Saku chose to become sterile a number of years ago so when it was discovered she was expecting, well you can only imagine what a scandal that was. They definitely believed love was worth risking everything for. I personally don't recommend it. The guard was killed right away and the girl was banished to some awful place."

Gabriela thought the story a strange one for Lyn to tell, or was this a warning of some kind? Lyn always had a reason for everything she said. "Now, what are these great ideas you have for me tonight?" Gabriela injected to change the subject.

"To become Saku's favorite is the best chance for you to find out what you need to discover." She said simply nodding her head. It was too dangerous to mention out loud what I was there to accomplish. Leonidas told me they estimated well over a thousand people would die or be imprisoned for life if and when they discovered Saku's list.

"I agree, Lyn. What are your ideas to secure me this special place in the harem?'

"You must do exactly as I say, regardless of how foolish it sounds to you. Remember, I have seen him through six or seven of these so-called harems. I know what keeps his attention. He wants a challenge, Gabriela. The other six girls think he is just with them for sex, but Saku can have all the high priced call girls he wants.

"When he visits them, they dress like vulgar, like, well I have to say it…sluts! He is looking for much more. He loves art, music, and horses. You see the art he loves, well, except for Klimt, of course! Horses? Over there are stacks of books for you to look through. Know enough about them to at least have good questions. But the music is what every girl gets wrong!"

"Music, I am sure to get that wrong. When I left home, my friends and I were dancin' to Michael Jackson's *Dangerous*.

"Oh, Lord, no! Mr. Saku is over sixty years old. He appreciates the talents of the new artists and has made a lot of money in his clubs and casinos with their music. But he is a diehard fan of Frank Sinatra."

"No way!"

"Oh, yes, I will not forget when Sinatra visited him in London. Saku was a nervous wreck. Believe me!" She said holding up a stack of CDs, "These will be your ticket.

"Wear a simple black dress, something Jackie O would wear, or Natalie Wood, his favorite actress of all times. You know Natalie Wood right? Or Jackie Kennedy?"

"I've heard of her," she mocked.

"I ordered dinner for you two. Play hard to get, be the one he has to work hard for. I shouldn't give you anymore advice for this evening; I need to let you settle in."

"When you said play hard to get, you mean for tonight?"

"For as long as you can! The longer you play him, the more he will want you. Trust me."

Gabriela did exactly as Lyn instructed and wore a simple black dress. He was to arrive at seven sharp. Dinner was coming at eight. Why on earth did Lyn make it so late? What were they going to do for an hour besides sip the champagne? She was anxious now; her hands shook as she tried to put on her pearl stud earrings. The black dress was sleeveless, "To show off those magnificent shoulders!" so Lyn thought anyway. It was very fitted and came just above her knees.

169

She walked into the entrance and stood watching the clock tick its last minute. Then straight up seven, there was a knock at her door.

"She unlocked the door and the guard opened it. There he was—Mr. Saku himself. Gabriela smiled and thought, *He doesn't look so much like a criminal just now*. He was not tall, a little round in the middle. His custom-made-to-fit-perfectly suit made the most of his looks. His hair was jet black with a tiny bit of gray. He smiled like a gentleman and asked if he could come in.

"Of course, I'm sorry, where are my manners? You see, I just moved into this place today and am still pretty unnerved by it all!" Saku roared with laughter.

"Ella Muñoz, I have heard about you for awhile now. Your photos have not done you justice. Muñoz with a *z*—that would be Spanish; your ancestors were originally from Spain?"

"My Grandmother Nuna said they were. But as you probably have heard, I am from Manila."

"I can already tell by those eyes of yours you are full of fire."

"That, Mr. Saku shall be determined by us both at some point. Let me take your coat and pour you a glass of champagne."

"I am comfortable enough with it on, but champagne would be good. So, you like Ella's Place?" he said with pride.

"I've never seen anything close to it. Even when I was visiting the Queen at Buckingham Palace last week, there was nothing as grand as this!"

"Oh, my dear girl, you are refreshing; beauty and a sense of humor?" then he thought to himself, *Can I also hope for intelligence?* They walked and talked about the décor. He enjoyed pointing out details in the paintings. Then, suddenly it was eight and dinner was served. While the waiter prepared the table, Gabriela put on the Sinatra CDs.

"Nice choice, I am extremely pleased with the music and with you."

They spoke during dinner about everything that was not important. Gabriela tried to find out what she could without prying. She focused on everything he said in hopes that something would be the clue she was there to discover.

It was 10:00 P.M. when he stood up from the table and said, "Delightful dinner and conversation."

Then he left, without even trying to kiss her. "I think Lyn is brilliant."

Clues

Mr. Saku came often to see Gabriela for over a month, each visit becoming more intimate. On his last visit, he gave her a sweet kiss, like one you would give a child at night. Lyn said he raved about her to all the staff. "She is fun and challenging, smart and inquisitive about everything." Leo was tormented hearing Saku congratulate him on his wonderful Filipino find. "Leo, she's one of the best ever, maybe only one other as good." Leo could barely tolerate these compliments, but when Saku began to describe what he intended to do to her very soon, Leo immediately found an emergency to tend to. A man in love can only take so much!

Gabriela spoke with Lyn every day. "Lyn, I've gotten nowhere with clues about Saku. He never wears anything twice. He has a different watch on each time I see him. No jewelry that he wears regularly. Maybe he has everything memorized."

"No, Gabriela, there can be no way. Leo says he has hundreds of bank accounts all over Asia and Europe. There has to be a place he has it stored. Keep looking. I think soon now you will have a chance to see everything. He has never waited this long to have one of his girls. Maybe then you will discover where he is hiding it."

Leo was hearing daily about more terrorization from Saku's thugs. Authorities were on alert, waiting to get some information from him. They must get names, cites, addresses, and banks. Whatever piece of information she could find would help. Leo could tell that Saku trusted her more each day. One detail Leonidas did not mention to Gabriela was when the big shake down came, he also would be charged. His name was on everything. Leonidas would definitely get locked up, he wasn't sure just how long. He felt he would be given leniency for his help in Saku's apprehension. But the truth is he had worked for and with Saku for seventeen long years. Leonidas did not mind this so much for himself but he was worried about how it would affect Gabriela.

When he started to get anxious, he would say to himself. "She knows I love her, we both chose this sacrifice." He touched his hand to his chest. He could feel the familiar silver cross that he had worn for years through his shirt and whispered, "He knew about sacrifice, too."

Gabriela thought about Leonidas throughout the lonely days waiting for Mr. Saku's visits. He had been patient with her so far, not pushing her at all. Then it was like he became someone completely different over night. It was a night she would never forget.

Saku was early for his visit with Gabriela that evening. He was impatient and rude at times. "Is everything all right, Mr. Saku? Have I irritated you in some way?"She asked timidly.

"Ella, I've had a hard day. I am under stress all the time. People think it's easy to be at the top, but it isn't. There are always those who want to betray you, to get your place at the top. I am in constant stress. My chest is always hurting."

"It's your heart isn't it? I've seen your nitro glycerin spray; my Grandmother Nuna had to use it, too."

"Well, I think my life is a bit more stressful than your grandmother's."

Gabriela knew he was behaving differently. Had she put him off too long, or perhaps found out about her mission? She spoke to ease her thoughts. "I can't imagine the stress you must endure. You provide me a life with no stress and I am thankful for that."

"Well, I think it's time to finally get what I have paid such a high price for. He walked over to Gabriela and ripped the front of her dress and started to kiss and bite at her neck, while pawing her with his hands. He was rough and aggressive, pulling her to the bedroom. He pushed her down on the bed and just as he started to climb on her, he grabbed at his chest and fell back.

"Oh, God, my chest…feels like a truck is on it." He was pulling at his shirt and gasping for air. "Get me help!"

"Where's your nitro spray?" she grabbed his coat in an effort to find it.

He yelled at her in irritated panic. "Call the guards, you damn fool! I'm dying, I don't need that!"

Gabriela ran to the door screaming for the guards. A deafening alarm went off. Men came from every direction. Four guards picked him up shouting out orders. Leo was there but never looked at Gabriela once. He was on the phone calling a doctor, she assumed. Then they were all gone. The alarm silenced and she stood alone with her torn dress clutching Mr. Saku's nitro spray. He just had a heart attack and said he didn't need this. She carefully removed the lid. She found hidden inside the container a titanium thumb drive to a computer. Gabriela smiled, knowing she had accomplished what she had been chosen for, discovering Mr. Saku's list. He was right; this would be of no use to a dying man. She picked up the phone and called Lyn.

Endings

Lyn came to her quickly. She knew Gabriela would need someone to talk to after the traumatic incident. "Lyn, it was so bizarre. He was acting differently from the moment he arrived. He was angry and agitated, almost cruel."

"I have heard of that type of behavior right before a heart attack. He was under stress; I overheard him tell Leonidas that he was leaving to meet the group later tonight. Something was going down wrong."

"Well, if it hasn't yet, I'm pretty sure it will as soon as Leonidas gets this!" She opened the nitro spray container and showed Lyn the thumb drive hidden inside.

"Oh, Gabriela, that's got to be it. He carried one of those things everywhere. No one ever asked him to give it up. Even going through security, it was medication. He was brilliant!"

"Not so brilliant to leave it here…with me!"

"You are right, not smart on his part, but a miracle for millions of others. I'll call Leo and he will know what to do with this information. We need to hurry just in case he comes back to get it, or sends someone."

"Yes, call Leonidas now."

Leonidas returned within the hour after making certain Saku was taken care of. His only concern about his condition was that he did not die before they had a chance to find his contact list. Thanks to Gabriela, it was found.

Saku died the next morning, never recovering from the massive heart attack. There was talk that someone had intentionally given him something to bring on his attack, but it could not be proven.

When Leonidas returned to Gabriela's suite, he took the thumb drive from her and hurried to his room. He then proceeded to download over four gigabytes of information from it. The drive contained names of ringleaders, drug lords, pimps, illegal arms and diamond smugglers; all identified with locations. Human trafficking was also stuck hard.

Hundreds of brothels were raided, pimps and sex traffickers were arrested, and children were released from their possessors. There were so many children found that numerous organizations were started to feed and educate them. New fines were placed on men caught paying for sex while the prostitutes were not punished. They were viewed more as victims than as criminals, since most of these women had no other means of supporting themselves.

But even that changed. Faith-based organizations joined with universities to start educating women, teaching them to provide for themselves. People were encouraged to give time and money to support organizations who trained men to think differently about women. They knew if men would stop paying money for sex with helpless young girls and children, the sex traffickers would be out of business. The small treasure that Gabriela found the night of Saku's heart attack was one of the biggest finds ever.

Beginnings

Soon after Saku's list was found, Lyn and Gabriela were told they had twenty-four hours to vacate the building. The building and everything in it was being confiscated by the authorities. They were given the opportunity to leave without being charged because of Gabriela's help. Leonidas was charged and put in prison to serve a ten years sentence for his involvement with Saku. Gabriela was free to use her real name but was advised to not return to Manila. Too many people had heard of her and ready to take revenge. However, she was able to get word to her family and prayed that maybe in time she could return home to them.

"Lyn what should I do now? I was told not to return to my family, and I am basically broke. I do have my Klimt that I could sell, but it would break my heart to do it."

"You are going with me."

"Where is that—to your daughters? Do you even know where they are?"

"I do now. Leonidas discovered from some information on the thumb drive that each of them had died. They lived in seclusion for so long the stress of it took them one by one."

"Lyn, all these years you and Leonidas stayed with Saku to save them? And all along they were not even alive? How could he have been so cruel to you both?"

"He wasn't about to let us know they were gone. I thought often they might be, but I didn't know for sure and wasn't willing to take a chance with their lives"

"I understand. That's what kept me quiet and submissive as well. So, you said I could go with you. Where is it we are going?"

"Well, like Leonidas has said to you so many times, there is one more thing that you need to know."

"More! What more?"

"Saku's family owns a large estate just outside of Tokyo."

"I am shocked it hasn't been confiscated with the rest of his properties."

"They cannot touch this particular property, it doesn't belong to him."

"You just said it belong to Saku's family."

"Yes, it does. Saku's father left his entire estate to his only grandson, keeping it in the Saku family, but not leaving it to his son, his grandson."

"Grandson?" Gabriela asked still confused.

"Yes, and that grandson is Leonidas!"

"Leonidas is Saku's son? How can that be? Lyn, who is Saku to you?"

"I was once one of the girls in his harem, over thirty-eight years ago. So long ago, it was before his lust for more turned him into a hardhearted evil man. I believe he cared for me more than he had cared for anyone before. I became pregnant and he allowed me to keep the baby; which was something he never allowed any of his harem to do. If a pregnancy occurred, it was terminated immediately. When our baby was born, it was a boy. I

177

named him Leonidas; a Greek name which means, 'remembrance of the Lord.' I was certain he was a gift from above."

"Saku was so elated that I had given him a son. He allowed me to have two more babies—both were girls. Soon after, he decided to become sterile. He had his son, that was enough for him. When Leonidas was eighteen, Saku decided it was time for him to become involved in his father's operations. Saku's dream was for his only son to take over the entire dynasty one day. Leonidas despised the things he had observed his father doing throughout his life, and outright refused Saku."

"Saku was outraged at his refusal. That's when Saku took the girls and forced us to stay and do whatever he told us to. I was assigned the job of training other girls for his harem and Leonidas was given the responsibility to find them."

"So, you are telling me, Leonidas, not Saku, inherited the estate in Japan? Did Leonidas even know about his inheritance?"

"Oh, yes, before his grandfather died he came and spoke with him, asking him to leave Hong Kong and come there to live with him. But Leonidas would not leave me, nor put his sister's lives in danger."

"So, this estate is there just sitting empty, waiting for Leonidas to claim it?"

"Yes, and a great deal of money as well!"

Gabriela sat down and then looked at her dear friend and said. "Please, tell me you have the keys!" Both of them had a good laugh and a good cry; then, freely, they walked out of Saku's building.

Gabriela stared proudly at her passport. It contained her photo with the name Gabriela Mendoza on it. Their flight just landed and they were now in Tokyo. She had never been to Japan, but it was to become her new home. She and Lyn got through customs without any trouble and Lyn was relieved. She said she would not be peaceful until they were both safe at the Saku estate. They had taken only a few things from their wardrobe closets, but none of the jewelry. Neither one wanted anything purchased with Saku's blood money. Lyn had sold some of her personal belongings to get them to Tokyo, but they knew the small amount of cash wouldn't last long. They just wanted to find their new home and feel safe.

They secured a driver at the airport who was familiar with the address Lyn gave him. "Oh, yes," he commented on the long drive there. "That estate is one of the loveliest in all of Japan." Gabriela loved hearing him speak, it reminded her of Maylin. "No one has lived there for many, many years! You go there to visit, or stay?"

"We are going there to stay." Lyn said with conviction.

"Ah, I see."

The drive was lovely; Japan was beautiful with green hills that protruded straight up out of the ground. It looked like a painting a small child would have drawn. There were fields of small vegetable gardens all perfectly planted in rows. It was cool, not hot and humid, which was a welcome change.

"There it is, Saku Estate!" reported the driver with pride. "Ah, yes, a lovely sight."

There was no denying it. A lovely sight was an understatement. It was perfection. As they entered the gate, they could see a large main house with several guest cottages surrounding it. A grand driveway led them to the front of the main house; a two-story grey stone with a commanding entrance. Japanese floral gardens were meticulously groomed along the walkway to the front door.

The driver stopped the car then got out and opened the taxi doors for the two women.

They stepped out of the car gazing at the commanding house in front of them. Gabriela paid their driver and they both walked toward the steps leading up to the front door. Lyn took the key in her hand and slipped it into the lock, then opened the door and they stepped inside.

The house was as the owners had left it, filled with beautiful but simple furnishings. Lyn took Gabriela by the hand and said, "You are home, Gabriela!"

Both of them knew it would take time to make it their home, but there were no locks on the doors or tyrant dictator holding them captive, just them and peace which filled the house. At the end of each day, Lyn would say good night to Gabriela and retire to her room. Then, Gabriela would climb the stairs and go to her room; open the window and look out at the moon and say, "Goodnight, Leonidas, I love you. Come home soon…I'll be waiting."

Appendage

Darcy thought of Gabriela, often wondering if she were safe. She would never forget her or what she had given to herself and the others in the tent room barracks. Darcy wished there was a way for her to know just how much! Darcy wouldn't have made it after her beating if Gabriela had not nursed her back to health. Since the escape from the barracks, Darcy had worked tirelessly with the underground, rescuing over three hundred other girls over the past ten years. Of course, the apprehension of the main ringleaders several years ago accelerated their efforts tremendously. There was talk about a young girl finding the list which had most of the leaders named along with all the incriminating evidence needed to convict and imprison most of them.

Because of Darcy's association with the underground, many of the girls rescued in the barrack's raid eventually made contact with her. Some joined the underground movement to give to others what they had been given—freedom. Others got jobs in restaurants, dress shops or worked as housekeepers or in healthcare facilities. The last she heard, Maylin moved to the U.S. with the businessman who purchased her. Soon after they arrived, she gave birth to a healthy baby boy. But the one Gabriela would be most proud of is her Kirima. Oh, what a gift Gabriela gave when she allowed Kirima to go free instead of herself.

After finding her daughter, she remained in the community she was from, living with a single mom and her children. Kirima was passionate to bring change to the way women were treated in her country; in time, she became one of the first females elected to the House of Representatives in India.

Darcy closed her eyes and spoke a prayer of thanksgiving for Gabriela and her idea of morning and evening circle. For it had been life changing for everyone—she certainly gave us *more than rice*.

FACT SHEET

1. Every 30 seconds another person becomes a victim.
2. 99% of victims are not rescued.
3. Approximately 2 to 4 million people are trafficked in and across borders each year.
4. Human trafficking is now a leading source of profits for organized crime, together with drugs and weapons, generating an estimated 9.5 billion dollars per year. – *US Department of State: Trafficking in Persons Report*, 2007
5. The overwhelming majority of those trafficked are women and children.
6. The average victim is forced to have sex up to 20 times a day.
7. The CIA calculates that profits from one trafficked woman alone average around $250,000 American dollars per year. – *Trafficking in Persons: U.S. Policy and Issues for Congress,* 2007
8. Children are abducted from rural areas and trafficked into a range of exploitive practices which include bonded labor, sexual exploitation, marriage, illicit adoptions, and begging.

9. Young girls, some as young as 12 years old, are forced to work in brothels, massage parlors, prostitution rings, strip clubs, or used to produce pornographic materials.
10. Children are recruited and trafficked to earn money by begging or selling goods.
11. Child beggars are sometimes maimed by their captors to generate sympathy and generosity from potential buyers.
    – www.thea21campaign.org/index.
    php/home/the-reason#_ftn1
12. Most victims of sexual exploitation and modern slavery are under 18 years of age – www.un.org/News/briefings/docs/2009/090212_UNODC.doc.htm
13. For every 75,000 victims, only 1 trafficker is convicted. – www.onevoicetoendslavery.com
14. 300,000 children in the U.S. are at risk every year for commercial sexual exploitation. – *U .S. Department of Justice*
15. An estimated 14,500 to 17,500 foreign nationals are trafficked into the United States each year. The number of U.S. citizens trafficked within the country is even higher, with an estimated 200,000 American children at risk for trafficking into the sex industry. – *U.S Department of Justice Report to Congress from Attorney General John Ashcroft on U.S. Government Efforts to Combat Trafficking in Persons*
16. An estimated 2.5 million children, the majority of them girls, are sexually exploited in the multibillion dollar commercial sex industry – *UNICEF*

Recommended reading materials:

1. *Not For Sale: The Return of the Global Slave Trade—and How We Can Fight It* - by David Bratstone (HarperCollins Publishers, 2007)
2. *The Natashas: Inside the New Global Sex Trade* - by Victor Malare (Viking Canada 2003)
3. *Terrify No More: Young Girls Held Captive and the Daring Undercover Operation to Win Their Freedom* - by Gary A. Haugen and Gregg Hunter (Thomas Nelson, 2010)
4. *The Road of Lost Innocence* - by Somaly Mam (Spiegel & Grau 2008)
5. *Human Trafficking* - by Joyce Hart (Rosen Publishing Group, 2009)
6. *Human Trafficking* - by Kathryn Cullen-Dupont (Facts on File, 2010)
7. *The Slave Next Door* - by Kevin Bales (University of California Press, 2009)
8. *Ending Slavery* - by Kevin Bales (University of California Press, 2008)
9. *Half the Sky: Turning Oppression into Opportunity for Women Worldwide* - by Nicholas D. Kristof and Sheryl WuDunn (Vintage, 2010)
10. *Sold* - by Patricia McCormick (Hyperion, 2006)

Recommended movies (for mature audiences only):

1. *Lilya 4-Ever (2002)*
2. *Human Trafficking (2005)*

3. *The Jammed (2007)*
4. *Trade (2007)*
5. *Taken (2008)*

How You Can Help

Get familiar with the crisis:
- Form a book club and read books about human trafficking.
- Raise awareness in your club, synagogue, church, and among your associates.
- Get the facts from the books and movies listed.
- Enlist the support of your friends with YouTube, Twitter, Facebook, blogs and all forms of social media.

Visit these web sites for the latest information:

www.equipandempower.org

www.onevoicetoendslavery.com

www.humantrafficking.org

www.notforsalecampaign.org

humantrafficking.change.org

www.theA21campaign.org/

www.demiandashton.org/

www.sharedhope.org/

www.polarisproject.org/

www.love146.org/

www.sctnow.org/

www.freetheslaves.net/

Take action:
1. Pray.
2. Lobby politicians at: www.polarisproject.com.
3. Organize a fundraiser. See what these college students are doing: www.tigersagainsttrafficking.com.
4. Support survivors: www.nightlightbangkok.com.
5. Use your talent to create a drama, short film, song, and share on: www.youtube.com.
6. Sponsor those at risk: www.compassion.com.
7. Motivate the media: encourage your local paper and television stations to cover trafficking stories.

Afterthoughts

Gabriela came face to face with a sobering truth on the day that Senagal, number nine, died. As she prepared rice and tea for the girls in the kitchen, in anger she asked God (whom she didn't even know if she believed in), "What are You going to do about this God?" Immediately, a voice came back at her with the heart wrenching question, "What are YOU going to do about this?" This question sums up the entire message of *More Than Rice*.

Every day, each of us go about our day not concerning ourselves with injustices and deep needs of others. We think that since we can't do anything big to change things, we shouldn't even attempt anything! But there are things we can do to change things in this world if we simply stop our busy, sometimes self inflicted, hectic lives for a moment... and do what we can.

I have listed on the following pages many ways to get involved in the fight against human trafficking. I encourage you to choose at least one and do it. But I also want to remind you that there are opportunities daily to make life better for others. Like Gabriela's daily ritual of preparing rice and tea for the girls, it may seem small, but small things done with love matter. So, the question to you is... what are YOU going to do today to make a difference in someone else's life? Please send me a message at www.twitter.com/more_than_rice if "Rice" has motivated you to some sort of action to change the world for the better.

Blessings on your efforts,
Pamala

LaVergne, TN USA
25 September 2010
198440LV00001B/2/P